THE BUSINESS OF CHANGING LIVES

How One Company Took the Information
Superhighway to the Inner City

ALLAN WEIS

with Valerie Andrews

GREENLEAF
BOOK GROUP PRESS

Published by Greenleaf Book Group Press
Austin, Texas
www.greenleafbookgroup.com

Distributed by Greenleaf Book Group LLC

For ordering information or special discounts for bulk purchases, please contact Greenleaf Book Group LLC at PO Box 91869, Austin, TX 78709, (512) 891-6100.

Design and composition by Greenleaf Book Group LLC
Cover design by Greenleaf Book Group LLC

Publisher's Cataloging-in-Publication Data
(Prepared by The Donohue Group, Inc.)

Weis, Allan H.
    The business of changing lives / Allan H. Weis with Valerie Andrews. -- 1st ed.

    p. ; cm.

    Includes bibliographical references.
    ISBN: 978-1-60832-011-0

    1. Advanced Network & Services--History. 2. Internet industry--United States--History. I. Andrews, Valerie. II. Title.

3 3988 10087 2768

HD9696.8.U6 A38 2009
338.7/6102504/0973   2009930303

Part of the Tree Neutral™ program, which offsets the number of trees consumed in the production and printing of this book by taking proactive steps, such as planting trees in direct proportion to the number of trees used: www.treeneutral.com

Printed in the United States of America on acid-free paper

09 10 11 12   10 9 8 7 6 5 4 3 2 1

First Edition

The real source of wealth and capital in this new era is not material things. It is the human mind, the human spirit, the human imagination, and our faith in the future.

Steve Forbes

CONTENTS

PREFACE

GIVING COMES NATURALLY TO MOST OF US, but social entrepreneurs want to give in a way that makes a lasting impact on society. After creating the backbone of the Internet, my company decided
to help young people around the world tap into the collaborative
power of networking. Advanced Network and Services (ANS) has
spent more than $128 million introducing students and researchers
around the world to the magic of computers and online learning, and
investments made by our partners in support of ANS took that number beyond $600 million. For the past twenty years, we've been in the
business of both creating new technology and changing lives.

As founder and CEO, I have led this company through three
incarnations. I have written this book to share that exciting history
with you. Part One tells how ANS and its partners drove the high-
tech revolution in much the same way Lockheed Martin propelled us
into space. It describes the unusual business model—working with
universities, research labs, government agencies, and corporations—
that enabled ANS to design and operate in record time the world's
largest and fastest part of the Internet—and to keep up with its phe-
nomenal growth. We set ANS up as a nonprofit organization, and
we funneled in excess of $60 million of our revenues back into the
infrastructure, improving the service for all.

Today this same approach can help us deal with other critical issues like energy independence, education, and health-care reform. As this book illustrates, corporations and public institutions don't have to work at cross-purposes, each group focusing on its short-term profits. Together they can work on long-term goals.

Part Two relates how ANS introduced a new generation to the magic of technology. In 1995, we entered the realm of education and began to introduce students of all ages and nationalities to the magic of computers and the Internet by launching ThinkQuest, an educational Olympics on the World Wide Web. This global contest encouraged kids to create their own websites, and it became the largest and fastest-growing educational initiative on the Internet. During its fourth year, ThinkQuest drew participants from 120 countries. With its generous awards and scholarships, it encouraged more students to enter science and technology. We showed how nonprofits could change our schools, working from the outside in, to impart twenty-first-century learning skills.

Although the United States jump-started the high-tech revolution, other countries have caught up quickly. Students in Finland, Singapore, and Belgium, for example, have surpassed American students in math, engineering, and science.[1] A recent National Academy of Sciences report to Congress, *Rising Above the Gathering Storm*, warns that our general competency in these areas has declined in the past few years. The authors of that report urge policy makers to find new ways to bolster American competitiveness.[2] To do that, we have to be sure that every student has access to technology. Computer literacy is no longer a luxury; it is a national priority.

Part Three answers the tantalizing question, How will technology transform learning in the future? Imagine a small area in your home called a telecubicle that engages all the senses and allows you to interact with colleagues at a distance. This three-dimensional space, combining virtual reality and real life, provides a learning platform akin to the holodeck in *Star Trek*. ANS led and funded the national initiative to develop sophisticated computer applications that allow us to simulate any environment we choose and then actually step into the frame and interact with it. Soon schoolchildren will be able to walk inside a computer model of a hydrogen atom and literally feel the force that holds its molecules together. The telecubicle is about to make the learning process more visceral and intuitive and enhance our ability to collaborate online.

Part Four of this book explores our philanthropic mission: closing the digital divide and bringing the benefits of technology to all. By the year 2000, there was a worrisome gap between the technologically privileged and the technologically destitute. So ANS began looking for ways to promote computer literacy in our inner cities. In 2004, we became social entrepreneurs, helping low-income youth find high-tech jobs and offering them incentives to start their own businesses. Instead of accepting proposals, ANS identified worthy organizations and then began to mentor them, using its contacts and business expertise instead of simply writing checks. We created a new set of rules for sustainable giving and got these organizations on the path to self-reliance in an amazingly short period of time.

ANS managed to change the lives of hundreds of thousands of young people around the world, thus getting the largest possible return for our investment. The lessons we have learned will help government agencies and other nonprofits leverage their assets and allocate them wisely in challenging economic times. We present three case studies that show how to help bring organizations to national prominence for an investment of less than $1 million.

As innovators in the realm of technology and social change, ANS staff have other important messages to deliver. First, we have discovered that partnerships between the public and private sectors can foster innovation and get big ideas to the marketplace faster than any other business model. Second, we believe that this country can remain a player in the global economy by focusing on education, teamwork, and problem solving. Third, we have shown that the United States can stem the rising tide of poverty by training young people in computer skills and entrepreneurship. We hope this book will become a manual for policy makers, educators, and nonprofit organizations that wish to invest in our country's future.

Part Five of this book tells why ANS made the decision not to create a self-perpetuating foundation but to go for broke and give all of our assets away. This section contains tips that will be useful to everyone from government policy makers to CEOs to community volunteers.

IBM chairman Louis Gerstner once observed that computers are magnificent problem-solving tools, but they can't replace compassion, love, and understanding. The ANS story is important because it also shows how we can build a bridge between our latest advances in technology and the dreams and aspirations of the human heart.

Allan Weis
Sarasota, Florida
May 10, 2009

PART ONE

Building the Backbone of the Internet

CHAPTER 1

WORKING AT THE BLEEDING EDGE

There are no rules here. We're just trying to accomplish something.

Thomas Edison

AS WE REFLECT ON THE INTERNET and its now-pervasive role in organizing information and making it readily available to all, we owe a great deal to one man: engineer, inventor, and former president of the Carnegie Institute Vannevar Bush. (In explaining his unusual first name, "Vannevar," he once said, "rhymes with achiever.") Bush set the stage for many of the most important innovations of the twentieth century, and his legacy extends from the development of atomic energy to the use of computers to enhance human memory to a clear view of the national importance of investing in science and technology. As early as 1945, in an article in the *Atlantic Monthly*, Bush described a "memex" device that would store, organize, and cross-reference information in books, records, and personal communications much as our iPhones, BlackBerrys, and laptops—each device exploiting the Internet—do today.

Bush was among the first to point out that one of the keys to economic success and national security is to invest in leadership in scientific and technological innovation. As director of the Office of Scientific Research and Development during World War II, Bush convinced our government to invest in new technology and to work closely with American industry and universities, a policy that ultimately led to the creation of the National Science Foundation (NSF) and the Internet.

EARLY NETWORKS AND PROTOCOLS

In 1969, the Department of Defense created the ARPANET to connect its funded researchers and developers across the country. The architects of this program wanted to promote collaboration and information sharing on projects ranging from new device technologies to space exploration to particle physics. The base protocols TCP/IP for the ARPANET came from the work of Bob Kahn and Vint Cerf, who later received a presidential medal for their contributions. This early network was a tortoise by today's standards, running at approximately 50 Kbits per second. But it drove invention—especially innovation in the key technologies for open networking—and therefore dramatically enhanced the rate of scientific progress.

Most universities and research labs used a version of UNIX. In mid-1983, the University of California–Berkeley shipped its new version of UNIX to the worldwide academic and research community—with the TCP/IP protocol suite included free in the box—and that changed the landscape forever. This software allowed researchers at universities to form small campus networks easily. It also created a need across the academic and research community that resulted in the formation of networks that more broadly interconnected the islands of university and research laboratories around the world.

Several years later, under the leadership of Erich Bloch, NSF concluded that it should invest in a major piece of information infrastructure—high-performance computing and networking.

In 1985, NSF created a network linking five of its funded super-computer centers. These, in turn, connected to other local research labs and nearby universities. Called the NSFNET, it ran on a home-made router called a fuzzball that transmitted data at 56 Kbits. Slow speeds, its popularity, and traffic jams made it nearly unusable. But a networking community grew, and soon there were more than a dozen regional computer networks.

Fast-forward ten years from that first network of five super-computer centers and the accuracy of this vision and the wisdom of this investment are obvious. By 1995, the Internet was used for everything from scientific research to many aspects of commerce, news delivery, music, and video distribution. With a doubling time of sixty days, it had become the fastest-growing communications medium in history.

Amazingly, the corporate giants who were trying in the mid-1980s to develop standards and protocols for the imminent digital communications age did not drive the initial phases of this explosive growth. Rather, the Internet's initial growth came from its users, mostly from research and academia, who in large part had no economic stake in the in-place proprietary communications networks. The roster of those driving the incremental, standards-based evolution into the digital data era included players such as AT&T, British Telecom, IBM, and Digital Equipment, each with its own protocols. In addition, many of the European countries invested in their own way of moving information from place to place.

In those early days, transferring large chunks of information was a slow business, like pouring honey in winter. With each company and each country relying on its own proprietary computer language, moving data from one machine to another was difficult. Having so many conflicting protocols was like having twenty people speaking different languages all at once. But the game was about to change.

Supporting NSFNET

In June 1987, Stephen Wolff, director of the Division of Networking and Communications Research at NSF, requested bids from the nation's top universities, engineering firms, and telecommunications companies. The new NSFNET would link eight universities and five supercomputer centers across the country and operate at 1.5 Mbits per second. This twenty-eight-fold jump in transmission speed would allow researchers to send the contents of a book from New York to California in just a fraction of a second. No one knew how to move data this fast.

At that time, my department at IBM served the nation's top research labs and universities, and we were eager to get involved. But this undertaking was so large, there was no way we could accomplish it alone.

Several universities were willing to partner with us. We chose the University of Michigan, where Doug Van Houweling, chairman of Merit, a consortium of universities with its own computer network, had a talent pool of engineers. He brought his top people to our research center in Yorktown Heights, New York, to see if we could design a new high-speed routing system for NSF.

In a single afternoon, our team sketched out a prototype that could outperform any known technology. They came up with a revolutionary design that used multiple computers hooked together by a communications ring, bit interleaves, and the equivalent of chewing gum.

John Armstrong, senior vice president of science and technology at IBM Research, saw the potential for information sharing on a national scale and agreed to help us build the routers. We then had to find a telephone company that could carry data at these crazy speeds. Former IBM executive Dick Liebhaber was now serving as MCI's chief technical officer and executive vice president. Liebhaber knew that if his company was going to grow, it would have to reinvent itself as a data carrier. He was also a risk taker who, within days, pledged

THE EVOLUTION OF SOCIAL NETWORKS

In recent years, the World Wide Web has changed the way we do business and altered our political campaigns. It has also increased the average number of people in any given social network.

The concept of a network has been with us for centuries, and it's useful to consider the evolution of that term.

In the Middle Ages, the heyday of guilds and handicrafts, a network referred to an open-weave technique that could produce anything from a knight's chain mail to a wall-length tapestry depicting a battle or a religious scene. Yet it also had a social meaning. Everything from armor to the walls of a castle or cathedral can be traced back to artisan collectives, a group of individuals who performed a highly specialized task.

In the Industrial Age, the term *network* referred to lines of transport, as in a network of railroads. This network became a backbone of commerce, enabling businesses to connect and distribute goods across entire regions.

Throughout the Cold War, an *intelligence network* served our national security by tracking, sub rosa, political and economic shifts in foreign countries. This network reflected how much we knew about other cultures, and how we divided them into friends and enemies.

In the Information Era, a network referred to a chain of radio or television broadcasting stations, and it became a way of communicating with the masses. And with the birth of the World Wide Web, a network became the basis for collaboration across economic and social boundaries. The present definition of *social network* is *any group of people who provide one another with mutual assistance and support.*

Networking will continue to transform our society in the years to come—helping us to find alternative sources of energy, reduce our carbon footprint, care for the environment, close the opportunity divide, and build a better world.

to invest in the infrastructure needed to support the NSFNET and agreed to price these services for us before they were built.

By August 1987, we had all our major players in place. IBM would provide $10 million in equipment and brainpower. MCI would give us an 85 percent discount on its communication lines. Merit would run the National Operations Center in Ann Arbor, and the state of Michigan would contribute $5 million from its fund for economic development.

The favored bidders had more advanced technology, yet we had a better bottom line. While our competitors' bids ranged between $25 million and $40 million, we proposed to do the job for slightly less than what NSF had in its budget—$14 million—noting that IBM and MCI would make up the difference with corporate contributions.

In early fall 1987, IBM Research's Armstrong backed our project as though we'd already won the NSF contract. The company's engineers went to work on the new router—called a T-1 for the new rate in transmission—and it was a lucky thing they did. By the time we got the official nod from NSF that November, we had only six months to debug our system and get it up and running. With increasing demands on the system, the entire network was about to collapse.

IBM engineer Barry Appleman was under enormous pressure to create the routers from available parts. "Our final design had over 4,000 parts," he recalls. "Only a few of them were custom built. When we were finished, the T-1 router was six feet tall and the width of a large refrigerator. Today, we can transmit a hundred times more data with technology the size of a pizza box." As Appleman tested the equipment, IBM's software team also had only a few weeks to create a program that would tie all elements of our design together.

Meanwhile, MCI was challenged by our nation's vast geography. Seventy-five percent of the U.S. population is concentrated within the first few hundred miles of either coast. MCI had facilities on each coast, but there was a huge operational gap in the center of the country. Within six months, the company had to extend its service area throughout the Midwest, installing copper lines and microwave towers in rural areas. "We got very good at putting up new towers," says Matthew Dovens, MCI's project manager. "But sometimes we'd finish the job then realize we were on the wrong side of the road and in the wrong farmer's field."

By now Merit was in a hiring frenzy. Van Houweling and his staff were training sixty computer science majors at the University of Michigan to fix any problems on the system, day and night. Because our equipment had to be separated from the university's, the grad students worked at cramped consoles inside metal cages.

For a while it was chaos at three locations—IBM, MCI, and Merit—but by July 1989 our team had installed thirteen routers across the country, connecting a large segment of the university and government research sites. We ran a full test of the network and set up a national help desk. In the process, we learned that good people become great when you give them the chance to build technology no one has ever seen before.

Yet there was another take-home message of even greater importance. We had created a new business model, where government and private industry joined together to foster large-scale innovation. No one was inhibited by the need to preserve existing assets or to protect market positions. Our team was free to leapfrog many of the complexities that would otherwise have hampered rapid growth. As a result, the team moved explosively faster, and within a few years the proprietary networks were history.

A NEW MODEL OF INNOVATION

Nearly three months after the operation started—in fall 1989—almost all of the American research community was online and the network was again strained to the breaking point. NSF now wanted to bump up both the number of sites and the network's transmission rate to 45 Mbits per second, a rate they called T-3. This was thirty times faster than T-1. This leap in technology would require a whole new approach. It would no longer be efficient to divide up the work among IBM, MCI, and Merit. A single organization had to be in charge, and I saw this as a golden opportunity.

In late September 1989, I sent a letter to Armstrong explaining that the time was right to set up a company that could meet this challenge, and I asked for IBM's support. This would be a tricky undertaking. IBM did not have a good history of spinning off new ventures, especially once its products interfered with the company's changing strategy. So I sought the advice of Jim McGroddy, a vice president at IBM Research. McGroddy was familiar with the challenges of pursuing R&D within a giant corporation. His paper "Raising Mice in an Elephant's Cage" is now a business school classic.[3]

"Companies like IBM are elephants," McGroddy warned. "They succeed by doing what they do well: managing and growing large businesses with a well-defined set of customers. The processes by which they do this are thoughtful and deliberate." Such companies change course slowly, only after the market or the culture has given them clear messages. But the innovators are like mice: they have to change course quickly in order to survive in hostile or rapidly changing environments.

Could I take IBM seed money, work with another giant like MCI, and still maintain control of my new company? The answer was yes . . . if the mouse could find a way to dance with the elephants.

Over the next several months, I spent hours studying nonprofits created by companies like VISA and Land O'Lakes to see if this structure might work for a high-tech start-up. There were two good reasons to move in this direction. One, as a nonprofit, our company could take seed money from IBM and MCI with no strings attached. Two, it would also be easier to work with the government labs and universities because we would all be operating on a similar financial model. This approach would give us the greatest freedom to innovate, yet it was so radical that few people within industry understood it. It would also allow us to make rapid advances in the months ahead.

Smoking Routers and Ice Swans

As Isaac Asimov observed, the first words after someone makes a scientific discovery are usually not "Eureka!" More often than not they are "That's funny . . . ," referring to some glitch in the experiment. While we were developing our business plan, small teams of engineers were working day and night on our next-generation router as a proof of concept.

In March 1990, we were scheduled to demonstrate this equipment at the "National Net" symposium in Washington, D.C. Al Gore, who was drafting the High Performance Computing and Communication Act, would be the keynote speaker. This bill contained the seed funds for what we now know as the Internet. We had to look good, but our prototype had a habit of dangerously overheating. Nevertheless, we had agreed to give a national demo before all the bugs were out.

My colleague Jordan Becker asked the L'Enfant Plaza Hotel for 220-volt feeds and extra air-conditioning, describing our project as a "trade show booth." We didn't think it necessary to mention the huge power consumption and heat dissipation problems we'd encountered in our early tests.

The day before the symposium, our display was so packed with cables, computers, and monitors that it resembled the inside of a space shuttle. When we fired up the router, the temperature in the room began to rise. When the mercury climbed past ninety degrees, we removed the ceiling tiles to dissipate the heat. When that didn't provide enough relief, we placed fans around the room and opened all the doors.

We had only a few hours to bring the temperature down. If we didn't, our equipment would burn out. Becker scoured the hotel looking for a portable air conditioner. No luck. At midnight, the room was still as hot as a Cajun grill. Then inspiration struck: The hotel kitchen had an oversized ice sculpture in the shape of a long-necked swan. Becker carted it back to the conference room and set up four big fans, each one blowing icy air directly on the router.

During his keynote address, Gore promised that his legislation would address the need for advanced technology "like the ice swans that are part of the network demo down the hall." Our "not quite ready for prime time" router was the butt of jokes, but once we got the cooling system sorted out, it became the driver of the Internet.

CHAPTER 2

THE ELEPHANT AND THE MOUSE
A NEW BUSINESS PARADIGM

Imagination is more important than knowledge.

Albert Einstein

BY FALL 1990, we had decided on our corporate structure. IBM's attorneys, Cravath, Swaine & Moore, presented us with a bill for half a million dollars and our new company, Advanced Network and Services (ANS), was born. It was the most expensive nonprofit start-up to date. The reason: Our attorneys weren't just dealing with a single entity but with a large-scale collaboration between the public and the private sectors. We had a maze of agreements involving IBM, MCI, Merit, and NSF, all designed to get maximum innovation with minimum intervention.

Both IBM and MCI helped ANS out of the gate with a total of $14 million in cash donations. They would benefit from early knowledge of the Internet but would have no direct control over our management. We also had a unique arrangement with NSF. My company would own the network that provided services to NSF, bearing the cost of operation and the risk of loss. Within a year, we planned to open the network up to commercial traffic, setting up a for-profit arm to handle business clients. But we also pledged to reinvest those profits to "enhance the network infrastructure and services." NSF's Wolff believed that this would be the best way to handle commercial use of the network and, at the same time, build a national resource.

Senator Gore's office sent out a press release announcing the formation of our company. "Just as private contractors helped build the Interstate [highway system]," he said, "this new corporation will help build the national information superhighways that today's Information Age demands." Our board of directors included top people in science and technology, education, and the media. But our office in Elmsford, New York, was a casual no-frills operation that set the tone for every dot-com start-up in the years to follow. For the first several weeks, we sat on upturned orange crates and shared a car phone to communicate with clients and suppliers.

CHOOSING ANS'S FIRST TEAM

My second in command, Becker, was only twenty-eight, but he had already achieved some impressive firsts. As a summer intern at IBM, he had found a way to put more memory on a chip. Later he worked with two Nobel Prize winners on the electron-scanning microscope. Kristin Mortensen, my assistant at IBM, also joined the company, as did Bob Harris, former comptroller of the IBM Credit Corporation, who would serve as our CFO. We also hired Jim Parker, former senior vice president of corporate development, planning, and law at Columbia Broadcasting System (CBS), as our chief counsel and secretary, and within a year we had attracted top people from the Internet talent pool and many from industry.

There's an old saying: "Engineers will go on forever if you let them. They never run out of ideas. They just run out of time." ANS avoided that pitfall by hiring people from the business side who were used to launching products in six months.

When we needed a code name to identify our company, we chose "Valluga," the name of an extreme ski peak in the Austrian Alps. Some runs on this mountain are so dangerous that even a minor mishap can mean sudden death. Valluga was a reminder that in the months ahead we'd face some impossible challenges and have to play at the outer edge of risk.

CHAPTER 3

WHO RULES THE INTERNET?

There is nothing more difficult to plan, more doubtful of success, nor more dangerous to management than the creation of a new system. For the initiator has the enmity of all who would profit by the preservation of the old institution and merely lukewarm defenders in those who gain by the new.

Niccolo Machiavelli

WORD GOT AROUND THAT ANS was creating the world's largest and fastest computer network, and in the fall months of 1991 we got our first offers of venture capital. "We don't want investors," we explained. "We take donations. For $5 million, you get a seat on our board and early knowledge of the Internet." The financiers didn't understand our nonprofit structure. When we made it clear that our goal wasn't to get rich, it was to have the freedom to build new technology, they walked away.

Next, two foreign telecommunications giants—Dutch PTT and Northern Telecom—wanted a stake in the company. They, too, were confused when we explained that our business model was based on donations, not investment. We had no problem turning these offers down. Our cash flow rapidly increased as we took on our first commercial clients.

The roster grew to include such Fortune 500 companies as Merck, Goldman Sachs, Bankers Trust, Chevron, Citicorp, Ford, Lockheed, and Union Carbide. We charged corporations a higher fee than we charged our academic customers, and we billed those corporations for the level of service they requested. We even invented a term for that: COMbits—COM for commercial and bits for the amount of data sent.

Our customers could connect at different speeds (56K, T-1, and T-3) for fees ranging from $13,000 to $600,000 annually. They could also purchase gateways that allowed them to function as middlemen, or Internet service providers (ISPs), and security products that were hacker proof.

ANS was now running the largest and fastest network in the world, serving NSF, the data processing and telecommunications industries, and hundreds of other networks. And customers paid for our services one year in advance.

Our methods of charging were controversial in the early 1990s, and the storm still rages in the debate over "network neutrality." Proponents of net neutrality insist that all users have the same level of access to the Internet; they make no distinction between high-bandwidth users and those who limit their activity to searches and email. Yet our model still persists and has solid precedents. Industries from FedEx to the U.S. Postal Service offer different levels of services and routinely charge a premium for faster routing. In the standard business model, premium users drive improvements to the infrastructure and raise the standard of service for all.

LIKE CHANGING THE ENGINES ON A 747 IN MIDAIR

As corporate America discovered the benefits of doing business online, traffic jams and outages increased. As our technical vice

HOW FAST IS FAST? A LESSON FROM LIGHT WAVES

In 1987, our nation's first network could send about two pages of typewritten text per second over a copper telephone wire. Engineers from IBM, Merit, and ANS boosted this speed almost 700-fold within three years, allowing scientists to share high-speed graphics and weather simulations over optical fibers.

When the universities started clamoring for more power to handle complex multimedia in 1993, we gave them another jump in speed and capacity. Today, physicians can share videos of medical procedures with no blips or breaks in the image. And scientists can collaborate on laboratory experiments in real time, with no appreciable transmission delays.

In 1996, universities and research labs were clamoring for a higher-speed version of the Internet, where they could continue to evolve new ideas. Internet2 was formed, and for five years, ANS staff served as the chief architects and engineers for this effort, creating a network for universities and research labs that operated at 622 Mbits per second. Information is now carried on a rainbow of light through a fiber thinner than a hair.

With this technology, scientists are able to push vast quantities of visual and sensory information around the globe.

In 2004, scientists at the California Institute of Technology (Caltech) and the European Organization for Nuclear Research (CERN, one of the finest particle physics labs in the world) set a new benchmark, transferring via Internet2 6.63 gigabits per second traveling between Geneva, Switzerland, and Pasadena, California—a distance of 9,800 miles. Ever since data started moving at light speed, we've become obsessed with quantity. Today's computers now have storage capacities for which the average person has no frame of reference.

In 2007, scientists using CERN's Large Hadron Collider in Geneva generated 15 petabytes of data as they tracked the behavior of subatomic particles. Only a handful of organizations in the world have computers that can store this kind of information. So what's a petabyte? According to techterms.com, "It's 10 to the 15th power, or 1,000,000,000,000,000 bytes . . . And no, it is not what you do to make a byte purr."[4]

president, Guy Almes, quipped in October 1991: "There are three kinds of death. There's heart death, there's brain death, and there's being off the network."

When we fielded sixty router crashes in a single day, which brought down different parts of the Internet, I stormed into Armstrong's office at IBM to vent my frustration.

He listened patiently as I described the chaos on the network. When I finally calmed down, he said, "Let's get to work."

Within an hour, two hundred engineers, scientists, and mathematicians were homing in on the problem. First they placed our routers in Faraday cages to be sure that they weren't affected by unusual electronic emissions. Then they disassembled our equipment and tested all the parts.

Each router had seven adapter cards linking it to the national network. A statistician eventually discovered a problem in the seventh card. When there was a big load on the system, it didn't get enough power, and so the network crashed. The solution: Remove that card and reconfigure all the routers. IBM engineer Bharath Kadaba played a key role in this process. "While the traffic was growing exponentially and the Internet was expanding in all directions, we had to upgrade our router technology and software and debug the system," he recalls. "We were still running the old T-1 network so we could shift the traffic to this level while we made adjustments. But that wasn't as easy as it sounds. It was like changing engines on a 747 while it's in midair."

WEAPONS-GRADE SECURITY

As if that problem wasn't enough, we discovered another variation on Murphy's Law: "Everything that can go wrong will go wrong—*all at once*." While we were working 24/7 to stabilize the network, every one of our officers and board members was undergoing a national security check. ANS had developed some new security products for our government and commercial clients, and our code was so sophisticated that we had to register with the Department of State as a munitions dealer.

Our corporate clients wouldn't go on the Internet without adequate protection—pharmaceutical firms like Merck didn't want their internal networks or their trade secrets exposed to the outside world—so we built the first encrypted virtual private networks that ran on top of the Internet. The problem was, we did too good a job. Our encryption was so sophisticated it was considered "weapons grade," an indication of just how powerful technology had become.

A BATTLE OF IDEOLOGIES

About this time, many of our academic colleagues from the regional networks decided to launch their own commercial networks. Bill Schrader, a computer scientist at Cornell, formed one of the first ISPs, called PSINet, in 1989.

In August 1991, Schrader approached ANS when he helped start the Commercial Internet Exchange (CIX) that he hoped would grow into a federation of ISPs. At that point, CIX had two other members, one in Virginia and one in California. To create an economy of scale, they agreed to carry one another's traffic at no charge.

CIX then asked ANS to join as well, hoping to expand its service. If we said no, CIX would have to invest more money in its infrastructure. If we said yes, we'd be giving CIX a free cross-country ride on ours. Because we already ran the world's largest and fastest network, we declined. The principals of CIX immediately cried "unfair practices" and asked their congressional representatives to investigate us, claiming that ANS was merely a front for two corporate giants,

IBM and MCI. We had failed to position our nonprofit structure properly in the creation of national infrastructure and would suffer for it in the months ahead.

Schrader compared himself to a Jedi knight, claiming he was fighting for the little guy. ANS, he said, was like the evil empire Darth Vader served because it had too long a reach. He openly criticized the agreement that allowed us to own and operate the network for NSF. Then he protested that our alliance with IBM gave us access to its national marketing group and to a field service that could install and maintain equipment from Paris to Peoria, while CIX members had to build these systems from scratch.

ANS quickly became the target for every other fledgling start-up in the field of networking. It didn't matter that we were putting millions back into the infrastructure or that we were using our commercial profits to help the regional networks grow. The Internet was expanding fast, and everybody wanted a piece of the action. Throughout the 1980s, the developers of the Internet worked in an environment of cooperation and mutual trust. By 1991, those ideals had been eclipsed by the dynamics of the marketplace.

A Battle in the Press

Our competitors started talking to the press, painting ANS as the sole beneficiary of government funding for the Internet. On December 19, 1991, for instance, the *New York Times* published an article in which Schrader and others questioned the preferred status of ANS, asking if the company had unfairly grabbed up an important national resource. Now that ANS had taken on commercial traffic, what was it doing with the profits?

We wrote to the *Times* to set the record straight, noting that ANS was a nonprofit with a single mission: to build a national resource. We paid for upgrades on the network. This arrangement benefited commercial networks like PSI as well as the networks run by the universities. We also noted that ANS had no magical hold over the market: Our competitors were free to set their own prices, and they were now selling access to their networks at 75 percent of our base quotes.

We corrected the impression that ANS was in any way a subsidiary of IBM or MCI, noting that although we had received start-up grants from these companies, they had no share in the business. We also explained why the network was privately owned. While ANS provided services to NSF, it bore the responsibility for maintaining and upgrading the network and also bore the risk of loss.

Hindsight is always twenty-twenty. By now we realized we had made a colossal mistake in the realm of public relations. We hadn't made the nature of our agreement broadly public. Nor had we disclosed just how many millions we were spending on improvements to the national and regional infrastructure.

We were also bucking the widespread assumption that whenever a company mixed altruistic and commercial goals, the profit motive would win out.

As 1991 drew to a close, we faced congressional hearings for unfair business practices, and our relationship with our chief supporters, IBM and MCI, began to cool as well.

The Cost of Being First

In March 1992, Van Houweling testified before Congress, noting the advantages of our business model. Partnerships among government, industry, and academia fostered innovation and technology transfer, and they made America stronger, he argued. The nation's technology push had been accelerated because ANS secured the support of industry, attracting contributions from IBM and MCI. This kind of collaboration was one of the goals of Al Gore's 1991 High Performance Computing and Communication Act.[5]

Members of CIX then came to the podium, insisting that the developmental stage of the Internet was over. The national network no longer needed government support and should be handed over to private enterprise. Other commercial networks, they insisted, would "have the capacity to offer T-3 service in the very near future" and were about to catch up with ANS.

Finally, MCI's competitors, AT&T and Sprint, argued that ANS had too large a market share and was beginning to look a lot like a monopoly. The word was singularly inappropriate because ANS was much smaller than any antitrust target in the past, with a staff of merely a hundred employees.

Suddenly our freewheeling firm was going to be mired down in the bogs of bureaucracy. Pushing for congressional hearings had been a clever move on the part of our competitors, who hoped to distract us from our day-to-day operations. We had been hanged in the court of innuendo and punished by our competition by diverting our energies. IBM's antitrust case in the 1980s had been so all-consuming that the company blinked while the market expanded. Fortunately, our review would be less draconian than that initiated by the Justice Department in that antitrust case. Nevertheless, if we weren't careful, it could impair our creativity in the months ahead.

CHAPTER 4

RIDING THE
NEXT WAVE

Creating a compelling new technology is so much harder than you think it will be . . . you're almost dead when you get to the other shore.

Steve Jobs

EARLY 1992 SAW A HUGE JUMP in commercial usage of the Internet. Many of our customers became ISPs and started to compete with us. New value-added networks started springing up to serve niche markets as well. Traffic on the Internet was now compounding at the rate of 11 percent a month, and the number of networks was doubling every year.

By now, ANS had offices in New York, Ann Arbor, Washington, San Francisco, Boston, and Seattle. As the competition heated up, our sales reps complained that they were losing major ground to MCI. We couldn't win that battle: Every time we bid for a job, we had to call the MCI sales staff to price out the lines. Because they knew about each job, MCI salespeople started showing up at our clients' offices on the same day we did, and we started losing revenue.

OPPORTUNITY, NOT CRISIS

We had just taken over Merit's operations center in Ann Arbor, and our cash reserves were sinking fast.

In late spring, our CFO, Harris, said: "We have $87,000 left in the bank, and we've got a burn rate of $2 million a month. I've borrowed some money to tide us over, but we're going to need a lot more."

The question was how to turn this crisis into an opportunity. All the telecommunications carriers were now investing in Internet technology. There had to be a way to take advantage of this trend.

Northern Telecom made data switches, but its equipment didn't take advantage of the characteristics of Internet traffic operating at higher speeds, so we called Gerry Butters, president of Northern Telecom, with a proposition. "We can redesign your switches so they work with this new technology. In return, ANS would like a donation of $5 million."

"All you have to do is convince my R&D people in Toronto," he said.

Butters sent a plane to take us to the lab the following day. When we arrived, Northern Telecom engineers had no idea why we'd come, and we had to lead them through our ideas step by step.

"We think there's a way to put more memory on the outbound side of your switch," we said. "Here's what we'd like to do . . ." Each time we suggested an innovation, the chief engineer brought a few more of his colleagues into our discussion.

By the end of the day, we had forty techies in the room, along with Northern Telecom's top management, and together we redesigned their equipment. In the months ahead, Northern Telecom made hundreds of millions on that switch, and ANS got the cash infusion it needed just to stay afloat.

TESTING THE WATERS IN EUROPE

Once we had some money in the bank, we turned our sights to Europe and began to promote the Internet abroad. In early 1992, we approached Hagen Hultzsch at Deutsche Telekom, and Colin Bell, a consultant to Britain's Cable and Wireless (C&W). Both men had the imagination to see what networking could do for European businesses, and they were eager to partner with us.

Deutsche Telekom had invested billions in information technology but was now confronting significant obstacles to pan-European collaboration. In Europe, the national telecommunications carriers had developed their own proprietary protocols. It was like standing in a time warp that took us back to the early days of data communications in the United States, when computer and telecommunications companies were creating incompatible products.

C&W was in a unique position, however. It was a self-contained global operation with optical cables running underneath three oceans. The firm owned and operated more than forty national telephone companies throughout the former British Empire, including island facilities from Bermuda to Bahrain. Its CEO, Gordon Owen, was a telecom engineer keenly interested in launching a worldwide data network.

Bell wisely noted that C&W wouldn't have to compete with the strong national telephone companies in Europe. Instead, it could become "the carrier of carriers," consolidating and transmitting everyone's data around the world, emerging as multinational corporations' "one stop" shopping center for online communications. C&W hired him to spearhead this initiative, and within weeks he'd signed preliminary agreements with ANS for consulting, with Digital for installation support, and with Cisco for new routers. American technology was about to go global. All that remained was the final wave of financing.

The project was ultimately scuppered, however, by internal politics. Owen became enmeshed in a power struggle with the company chairman, Lord David Young, who failed to appreciate the economic power of the Internet. By the summer, the project was tabled, and we decided to try an alternative: We lobbied the European Union (EU) in the hope that it would adopt a universal platform for the Internet.

Lobbying for American Technology

In September, Bell and I went to Brussels to talk with Michel Carpentier, commissioner of the Industrial Directorate for Information Technology. In particular, we described the synergy between American research labs and universities and the commercial sphere. "Europeans should look seriously at this model," Bell said. "It's incredibly powerful and productive. People come out of universities to start new companies and keep America on the cutting edge of new technology.

"The Internet is about to change the way we do business," he added. "If you follow the lead of ANS and start building a strong network here, you can stimulate a whole new wave of economic growth."

Members of the EU defense community wanted to know all about the confidential work ANS had done for government agencies back home. But the industrial directorate had little interest in American technology, and they came up with an astounding proposition. Denmark had recently voted to leave the EU, which had devised a plan to try and win them back. "We will support your proposal to expand the Internet here," they said, "provided it is based on Danish technology."

"But there is no such thing!" Bell retorted. At that time, the Danish government was using outdated computers, and the country had little expertise in the Internet. Bell was so frustrated by the EU's display of provincialism that he threw up his hands and said, "They bring the mentality of the parish pump to the destiny of a continent!"

The European officials were struggling to balance too many political agendas in their attempt to advance Internet technology. The R&D community in Europe would suffer from their shortsightedness, and Bell and I left Brussels wishing we could have done more. In a matter of months, our plans to promote European networking had gone up in smoke. Yet there were still some things to be salvaged from the embers.

First, our lobbying called attention to several issues that needed to be addressed in Europe: competition among vested interests, fragmentation of protocols, a failure to grasp the economic power of this new medium. Second, ANS benefited from this adventure: We gained thirty new clients, all of them large European corporations that couldn't afford to wait for their governments to solve these problems on their own.

CHAPTER 5

MISSION ACCOMPLISHED

Genius is knowing when to stop.

Charles de Gaulle

BACK IN THE UNITED STATES, things were looking up. We finally received recognition for our contributions to the Internet and for our nonprofit structure. In spring 1993, one year after the congressional hearings, ANS went from being an industry villain to an industry hero. The government inspectors had submitted their report, giving us high marks. They understood the financial and technical risks we had taken and said that the technology we had created rightfully belonged to us. They noted that ANS had provided a valuable service to NSF, the academic community, and industry. Their audit showed that ANS had poured more than $50 million into upgrades of the network, stimulating the growth of the Internet.

A NEW ERA IN GLOBAL COMMUNICATIONS

The big surprise came later on, as our corporate allies did their own tallies. Both IBM and MCI had spent far more building this national network than was widely known. IBM's contributions alone totaled $150 million over the course of seven years, while MCI's were in excess of $200 million. In addition, MCI spent well over $2 billion just to improve its high-speed data capability.

In the long run, ANS received public commendation for drawing corporate support, running a state-of-the-art network, and helping launch a new era in global communications.

Under our aegis, commercial use of the Internet had gone from zero to dominant. In less than a decade, the Internet backbone had connected some 20,000 domestic and 24,000 foreign networks, with 20-million-plus users. And, while many of the foreign networks failed to adopt open source protocol, we found ways to accommodate their different communications protocols and create new economies of scale.

FINDING SUITABLE PARTNERS

Early in 1994 we faced a new problem. Our feisty start-up was in danger of turning into the establishment. There was little room for innovation, and our main task was hanging on to our market share. Board member Joe Dionne then gave us some sage advice. As chairman and CEO of McGraw-Hill, Dionne understood how companies evolve. The firm that opens up the market, he said, doesn't always survive its growth.

The market was also twisting in unexpected ways. In the years ahead, in order to be competitive, ISPs would have to "own" the underlying telecommunications infrastructure and the real estate that held their critical equipment. In retrospect, this has proven to be the case.

Our CFO, Harris, pointed out that ANS was now in a good position to attract a strategic equity placement. His idea was to find one or two new partners with both capital and technical expertise to share our responsibilities and help us run the network. Then we would have time to take on more exciting projects. The board agreed this was a logical next step and asked Salomon Brothers to help us identify a few potential candidates. Their presentation was elegantly simple:

- ANS was the recognized leader in the Internet.
- It owned the only high-speed T-3 network in the world.
- It introduced volume-sensitive pricing to the industry.
- It created sophisticated security products.
- It achieved a very high customer satisfaction ratings including an unheard of 100 percent for understanding customer needs.

By June 1994, we had twenty-six interested parties, including regional Bell companies, European phone companies, and venture capital firms. One of our top bidders dropped out when he discovered that the deal included the ANS technical staff but not its CEO.

In July, Steve Case, the chairman and CEO of America Online (AOL), made an offer to buy ANS's technical operations and commercial assets outright for $20 million in cash and $15 million in AOL stock. We accepted. As AOL stock shot up in value, the nonprofit arm of ANS ended up with $43 million. (We invested that money, and over the years, those investments would produce an additional $33 million in gains, dividends, and interest.) The question was, What to do with all this money?

It was time to focus on the future. By the end of the year, ANS had taken on a new mission: introducing a whole new generation to the magic of the Internet.

PART TWO

An Educational Olympics on the Web

CHAPTER 6

A NEW MODEL OF EDUCATION

In times of change, learners inherit the earth, while the learned find themselves equipped to deal with a world that no longer exists.
Eric Hoffer

IN 1995, MOST SCHOOLS were still working on a very old model, teaching students to memorize, perform routine tasks, follow instructions, and think *inside* the box. We were preparing our children for a world that would no longer exist by the time they graduated. The economy had gone globals, and the best-paying jobs were information based.

Children not only had to be familiar with computers, they also needed a crash course in "learning how to learn" so they could keep up with the evolution of technology and with the global marketplace.

In the late 1980s, the National Research Council's Panel on Information Technology and Conduct of Research first called our attention to the need to bring computers, and the budding Internet, into the classroom. ANS responded to that alert by deciding, in 1992, to connect a few schools to the Internet just to see what children could do.

CONNECTING STUDENTS THROUGH COMPUTERS

We began with a high school in Seattle. When asked to do a paper on World War II, the sophomore class turned, as usual, to the *Encyclopedia Britannica*. Yet one enterprising teen searched the online databases in Japan and found first-person accounts of the bombing of Hiroshima. This was no mean feat in the days before search engines. The other students then learned that they, too, could access primary sources online and explore history through the moving stories of eye-witnesses.

The next year, we gave some computers to a school in Harlem. The administration had no money to hire a tech adviser, so the students set up their own computer lab in an abandoned building and put the word out to the local gangs that the project was off limits. As the students learned how to use and maintain their computers, we gave them additional software and tech support. By the end of the year, their lives had been transformed. Teens who were in danger of dropping out were now engaged in academics and enjoyed new respect from their teachers and their peers alike.

In 1995, we asked many of the country's leading educators how to structure a contest that would encourage students to create new and exciting content on the Internet. One of our early contacts was Margaret Riel, who in the early 1980s launched the Intercultural Learning Network, which linked schools in Alaska, California, Japan, Israel, and Mexico. This project was run on an astonishingly low budget and used only five computers.

The students weren't on the Internet, but their local universities were. "We'd transmit the assignments from one university to the next," Riel explained. "And one of our representatives would bring the material to the school the next day on a floppy disk. Because we had to work around so many limitations, we called our program 'The Sneaker Net.'"

Riel took this prototype to AT&T and started the Long Distance Learning Network, matching up students and teachers around the world via telephone modems so they could work on independent study projects.

"We set up a system of computer pals, just like pen pals," she told me. "But it didn't work that well. When kids dropped out, we lost their partners as well, and our failure rate doubled. So we started organizing kids into groups. If one person lost interest, the others would carry on and the project would get finished."

By the early 1990s, the Long Distance Learning Network was serving better than thirty thousand students in one computer session. The project was expensive: AT&T had to send teams around the country to enroll the schools and put the technology in place. But with the birth of the World Wide Web, the technology was free, and anyone could play.

LAUNCHING THINKQUEST

By 1995, after talking to hundreds of educators—few with similar opinions—we had designed a contest called ThinkQuest that would encourage students to create their own websites. Students would work in teams, and we would start in the United States to be sure we had the formula right before going international.

ThinkQuest would also focus on the product development cycle—something most schools did not teach. Business skills would be built into the contest such that the students wouldn't even realize they were learning these skills. They would just be part of the process.

Riel compared the ThinkQuest teams to quality circles in the business world. "Kids will learn how to check each other's work," she said. "They'll refine their approach until they get the best result. But how are you going to hook them in?"

The answer was simple. We'd start by offering generous college scholarships to the top one hundred students. We'd give cash awards to the coaches and the participating schools. Although initially the contest would foster interest in math and science, we'd open it up to other academic categories as well. We also planned to provide software and training for the teachers.

To get the schools involved, we turned to Dr. Linda Roberts, director of the Clinton administration's newly formed Office of Educational Technology. Roberts explained that less than a third of U.S. schools had Internet access, and less than 3 percent of the teachers were using computers in the classroom.[6] At this point, there were no educational tools for the Web.

"We have so much to accomplish," she said. "We need to get the schools connected, support the teachers, and get good educational content on the Internet."

"There is a way to do that," we said encouragingly. "We can get students to build educational websites for their peers. They can teach each other how to use technology, and our guess is that they'll take to it pretty fast." We outlined the ideas behind ThinkQuest and told her that ANS had the funds to back it.

ThinkQuest's Unique Features

"The competition will be like the Westinghouse Talent Search," we said, "but with some important differences. We won't just target the best and brightest. We'll reach out to kids in inner cities and rural communities, and their results will be on the Web for years. We'll also encourage more girls to participate in math and science. The contest will be flexible. We can make it that way. We can give more points toward winning for things like collaborating with other schools, or with kids from low-income neighborhoods."

All of our decisions, I added, would be based on a single four-letter word—K-I-D-S.

BEYOND "USER FRIENDLY"

Technology is no longer about who has the latest gadget. It's about creating a web of supportive relationships.

As John Naisbitt predicted two decades ago in *Megatrends*, technology is at last evolving "from high-tech to high-touch." We've gone from geek speak—an early alphabet soup of terms including LANs and IPs and BPGs and HTML codes—to user-friendly programs, chat rooms, and emoticons, and online venues that allow us to describe who we are and what we value most.

In the past two decades, technology has become less about machines and more about the people who are using it. And that will be more evident as we move into Act II of the Information Age.

Today, one of the most rapidly growing activities on the Web is people reaching out and helping others. Online giving is on the rise, not just among adults but among the younger set as well. ThinkQuest students are designing websites for their favorite charities. And high school classes are logging onto sites like Kiva.org, where, with one click and a credit card, they can make micro-loans from $20 to $2,000 to support small businesses in the developing world from Tajikstan to Tanzania.

Thanks to the Internet, the average citizen can also participate in our great scientific quests. Grid computing allows you to link your desktop to a university mainframe and perform mega-calculations for a variety of research projects. You can join the Search for Extraterrestrials (SETI) community at SETI.org to analyze the random signals we receive from outer space. Or hook up with the World Community Grid (www.worldcommunitygrid.org) and find new ways to conquer cancer, dengue fever, and AIDS. In one project sponsored by this organization, scientists identified in just three months forty-four potential treatments to fight the deadly smallpox disease. Without the aid of grid computing, it would have taken those scientists an entire year.

It was easy to tell from the way Roberts' face lit up that this was something she liked and could support. She was most enthusiastic about ThinkQuest's focus on group and project learning. The kids themselves would figure out the best way to teach a subject—economics, math, science, literature, or history—and then they'd create an online library for their peers. Roberts felt this project would empower kids and give them their first real taste of independent learning. They'd choose a topic, research it, become "experts," and then start to mentor one another. Along the way, they would become Web masters.

An enthusiastic supporter, Roberts directed us to education listservs and advised me to start promoting the contest online. She also introduced us to her associate, Gwen Solomon, who became one of our key advisers. In the early 1990s, Solomon had founded New York City's School for the Future. What she discovered was pretty interesting. "Kids hate to be talked at," she said. "They learn best from doing things, working with other kids, and building on the strengths of others. When we let them take charge, they become the experts. That changes the whole framework of learning. This approach works just as well with special-ed and at-risk students as it does with those at the top of the class."

With the help of Solomon and a growing list of experts in the field, I came up with a comprehensive set of goals for the contest. ThinkQuest would:

- Foster collaboration among students, including those from different schools and different economic backgrounds;
- Encourage kids to teach their favorite subjects and explore ideas they were concerned with in their daily lives;
- Build an Internet library of high-quality educational websites embracing all disciplines—a series of active websites where students could help one another learn; and
- Reach out to kids in inner cities and remote areas who had little access to technology.

We also recognized that this generation's learning style had already been shaped by access to technology, from Nintendo to PC games. Kids are multitaskers and are able to think on several different levels at a time. Working on the Internet would hone these capabilities and create a new platform for twenty-first-century learning.

From Sage on the Stage to Guide on the Side

As we were designing the contest, I confessed to Solomon that I had a personal motive for engaging in this kind of work. I understood why kids tuned out in middle school because that's what I did as well. Though I came from a high-achieving family—my father was a stockbroker and a champion-level bridge player—I was a very poor student. The reason: I was bored. I hated copying notes from the blackboard and listening to endless lectures. Like most engineers, I was a born tinkerer and much preferred working things out for myself. How did I manage to graduate? I passed the Regents Exams required by New York State after reading the textbooks the night before the test.

My goal with ThinkQuest was to change the old model of education. To replace the "Sage on the Stage," who kept on talking whether the kids were connecting or not, with a "Guide on the Side," a coach or mentor who would encourage them to work independently and access their own creativity.

CONVINCING THE BOARD

By the time the ANS board met in September 1995, I had talked to the nation's leading educators and we were ready to pull out all the stops. We'd start by sending a ThinkQuest mailer to every school in America. Then, with a proof of concept, we could take the contest global. This would be easy with the international contacts we had developed at IBM and, later, as the builder of the world's largest computer network.

Some board members thought we were moving too far from our core competence in commercial networking. I countered that this project would draw on everything we had learned from building the Internet and would teach the next generation about collaboration and problem solving.

Others were skeptical that kids would be willing to devote their free time to building websites. But we had a ready answer for that as well. An educational organization called Global SchoolNet proved that students were highly motivated to engage in after-school programs.

Many on the board wanted to work with curriculum planners and local school boards. Yet I wanted to give kids a creative forum of their own—outside the system. "They can research and write the content, design websites, and make them interactive," I said. "They'll also have to figure out how to reach the widest possible audience. What could be better preparation for the business world?"

I met with ANS board members individually throughout October, explaining why ThinkQuest would benefit all students, not just future scientists and engineers. We'd give awards in all academic disciplines, and we'd show students how all professions could benefit from computer networking.

"We've just launched the world's most powerful communications medium," I reminded everyone. "Is there anything more important than teaching the next generation how to use it? Forget the old track system of college prep versus vocational school. In the next five years, American kids from all backgrounds will be competing for jobs on the Internet."

By November, the board voted to embark on this new adventure and invest our remaining capital in kids. The company was ready to take on a new challenge, and I was ready to be a new kind of CEO. At fifty-six, I no longer cared about capturing market share and finding ways to beat the competition. We had made our fortune on the Internet. Now it was time to use it to help kids benefit from the technology we created. As the playwright Thornton Wilder said, "Money is like manure; it's not worth a thing unless it's spread around encouraging young things to grow."

CHAPTER 7

THINKQUEST IS BORN

The number-one benefit of information technology is that it empowers people. It lets them be creative and learn things they didn't think they could learn before.

Steve Ballmer

IN DECEMBER 1995, we launched ThinkQuest from the Clinton White House, and by spring 1996, we had more than a thousand teams registered from forty-nine states.

Yvonne Andres, from Global SchoolNet, and Gwen Solomon organized in excess of a hundred education seminars across the country to show teachers how to incorporate the contest into their classrooms. These workshops gave us valuable feedback. Some teachers worried about how they could possibly fit another subject— computers—into an already crowded day. Others reacted to the new technology with the equivalent of "math anxiety," and many were concerned about losing their authority in the classroom, knowing that in the tech world, kids could easily outpace them.

In our seminars, we reassured the educators that they didn't have to become computer experts. Their job was to be facilitators. "The students are going to have a faster learning curve," our instructors said, "but that's going to free you up and let you concentrate on content. All you need to do is support their creativity."

Schools with newly formed tech departments readily embraced ThinkQuest. Dr. Beverly Rogers promoted the contest through the Texas Computer Education Association, running outreach programs for school boards and principals. Even though Florida and Alaska had their own educational computer networks, ThinkQuest provided them with a perfect platform for online learning.

THINKQUEST BASICS

The rules were simple: The contest was open to students in grades seven through twelve who worked in teams of two or three. Extra points were given for collaboration with other schools, for teams with mixed gender, and for mentoring students who had little access to technology. A ThinkQuest coach had to oversee the work at each location. In January, the teams chose their subject. They then had until July to design their websites and post their entries on our server.

Awards would be given in five areas: math and science, arts and literature, social sciences, health and sports, and an interdisciplinary category that allowed students to combine topics from two or more areas. The most impressive entry overall would be dubbed Best of Contest.

In the first year of the contest, our "hands-off" policy worked quite well. The kids had stunning ideas. All they needed was computer access and some adult encouragement. Don Hyatt, a computer science teacher at Thomas Jefferson High School in Alexandria, Virginia, opened up the computer lab on weekends and school holidays and served as a general sounding board. Other teachers followed his example. Parents and grandparents also served as coaches, providing home computers and snacks to keep up the students' energy.

For judges, we turned to the Internet Society, a respected and impartial resource. Their administrator, Lisa Ernst, assembled a blue-ribbon panel consisting of computer scientists, library media specialists, and educators with expertise in every category.

The judges scored each entry according to these guidelines:

- Does this website foster collaboration among students from dissimilar schools?
- Is the content fun, exciting, and of high quality?
- Is this an innovative educational tool?
- Is the website interactive, and does it draw other students in?
- Is the website used by many others as an educational resource?
- Does this website become more valuable as it is used by others?

"The entries were so good and the topics so broad and wide-ranging," said judge Kathy Schrock, a school librarian from Nauset, Massachusetts, "it was difficult to pick the winners."

In November 1996, we flew 101 ThinkQuest finalists and their coaches to Washington, D.C., for a lavish awards ceremony. "Educators were used to conferences run on a shoestring budget," recalls Solomon. "This time, they had private rooms and first-class accommodations. We wined and dined them, gave them demonstrations of the latest technology and a VIP tour of the nation's capital."

After communicating for months by phone or email, ThinkQuest students had the opportunity to meet their teammates from other schools. We set up a huge computer lab so finalists could show off their websites and explain how they chose their topics, researched them, and interviewed the sources. Soon educators and students alike were trading tips on web design and exchanging ideas for improving the next year's entries.

FROM WALL STREET TO WAR ZONES

If the judges were surprised at the educational content of the ThinkQuest websites, we at ANS were bowled over by their sophisticated graphics and high level of interactivity. Best of Contest went to *EduStock*, a Wall Street website created by a team from Potomac, Maryland. The daily workings of the stock market came alive with an investment tutorial and a simulator that allowed students to manage a portfolio.

"Get a real idea of what the stock market is like, and how much money you can make with stock investments," the students wrote, little knowing that they were introducing a tool that would revolutionize stock trading. "The data is delayed by only 20 minutes and is updated every time you use it."

EduStock became so popular that it was used for many years to teach economics from middle school through college.

First place in math and science went to *The Fractory*, an interactive tool for exploring fractals, or irregular geometric shapes, and their role in such things as astronomical events, car crashes, and the weather. Scientists had only just started to map these unusual patterns with the advanced calculating power of computers.

"Graph the weather over the past ten years, and what do you get?" the students wrote on their home page. "A seemingly random set of fluctuations that apparently cannot be represented by an equation. This is called chaos. There appears to be no pattern, and the only way to say for sure where the graph will be in the future is to continue graphing iterations, i.e., to predict tomorrow's weather perfectly you have to wait until tomorrow! At first glance, fractals seem the same way. They are extremely complex, and they appear to have a random shape. But many fractals are generated through simple mathematical equations!"

The enthusiastic use of exclamation points was the only indication that this website was created by kids at the Rocky Run Middle School in Chantilly, Virginia, not by graduate students at Stanford or MIT. The website showed how fractals can help predict seemingly random occurrences, and it allowed users to generate their own images of these patterns found in nature.

The interdisciplinary award went to students from Thomas Jefferson High School in Alexandria, Virginia, and West Anchorage High School in Alaska for a website on computer art, called the *Online POV Ray Tutorial.* "Download the free program," they promised, "and soon you'll be making exciting visual art" with Escher-like patterns, shimmering surfaces, and metallic hues. This program also showed other teams how to make their websites more visually appealing, illustrating one of the main principles of the ThinkQuest contest: Students could teach one another how to improve their entries every year.

Don Hyatt's computer lab in Alexandria, Virginia, produced an entry so advanced the judges begged us to create a special award for it, so we did. *From the Ground Up: A Guide to* C++ offered a step-by-step tutorial in computer programming that made it far easier for novices to enter the contest. Our early ThinkQuest teams didn't have Dreamweaver or any of the content management tools that allow us to create websites with such ease today.

These kids had to unravel the mystery of technology themselves. In the first year, one ThinkQuest team figured out html by downloading a website and looking at the code embedded in the text. After creating their own "Html Cheat Sheet," they proceeded to program their entries. The C++ tutorial, and other student-designed resources, made writing code a lot easier.

The most provocative entry in 1996, *War Eyes,* presented moving accounts of civil war, gang killings, and domestic violence in trouble spots throughout the world. What started out to be a play on words, "A Site for War Eyes," evolved into the project's title. "Those of us who have been touched by war are the War Eyes of this century and centuries to come," wrote these students from New York. "Whether it is gang war, civil war, territorial war, or world war, each human who has experienced war has been influenced psychologically . . . We believe that each of these stories has greater value if it can be shared."

NOT JUST FOR COMPUTER NERDS

ThinkQuest wasn't just for math geniuses or those familiar with computers. Its goal was to reach across all disciplines and to show young people that technology could help them master any subject they set their minds to.

Jennifer Grey, from West Lebanon, New Hampshire, was the moving force behind *Runner's Oasis*. Collaborating with students in Essex Junction, Vermont, and Garden City, New York, she took users on a virtual run, covering everything from athletic shoes to preparation for a marathon.

Texas students created a game to teach younger children about their local history. *The Mysteries of Los Caminos Reales* invited grade-school students to "explore a cave and look for forgotten treasure. Learn about wildlife, plants, Indians, and missions along the highway route."

A team from New Jersey took first place in social sciences, with *Anatomy of a Murder: A Trip Through Our Justice System*. "If you don't know your *habeas corpus* from your *voir dire*, take a closer look at the American justice system at this web page. Follow a mysterious fictional murder case through the court system as you learn all about grand juries, indictments, and plea bargains. Examine famous Supreme Court decisions and consult the 'Glossary for the Baffled' whenever the legalese becomes too much."

Finalists from Honolulu created an online game called *Design Paradise*, asking, How do you preserve natural resources and address a region's need for economic development? "The island of Kauai is a beautiful place with a natural rain forest, warm beaches, agriculture, and towns. As CEO of a major company, you must balance the needs of industry, environment, and population to create a stable and prosperous economy."

ThinkQuest participants also produced a website on *Teen Court*, an Illinois program that gave youth offenders a chance to clear their records. Inspired by the tragic story of a student who committed suicide after being arrested for a minor offense, Teen Court directs cases away from the juvenile courts, providing an alternative approach to litigating traffic violations involving underage driving, speeding, and alcohol use. The ThinkQuest team showed how to replicate this program and taught students how to hold their own mock trials.

War Eyes gained international attention as teens from Africa and the Middle East described their experiences of civil war and inner-city kids told how they dealt with violence in their homes and neighborhoods. For many, this website was a lifeline, a way of connecting to others who had witnessed death, loss, imprisonment, and even genocide.

Larry Landweber, president of the Internet Society, wagered that I'd break down in tears at some point during our first awards ceremony. When we got to *War Eyes*, he won his bet. *War Eyes* was the very heart of ThinkQuest—offering hope to young people who were struggling for survival in every corner of the world.

This website also grew in value as others used it. Books don't evolve to reflect the experience of their readers, but we were entering a new social era on the Net where websites encouraged a free and open exchange of ideas. *War Eyes* was the first of many entries that managed to reach out and change the lives of others.

THE THINKQUEST CREDO

From the start, ThinkQuest emphasized collaboration and problem solving. To build their websites, students had to deal with disagreements and overcome their differences with grace and tact. As one winner told me years later, the contest gave him hands-on training in diplomacy. "ThinkQuest was a valuable education in how to disagree constructively and how to negotiate with others. I'm using those skills as a small-town attorney, dealing with different kinds of people every day."

ThinkQuest also taught kids to respect and rely on one another's talents. Building a website required at least three kinds of expertise: Students had to research the topic, interview the experts, and write the content. They also had to provide the graphics and produce compelling illustrations. They had to program the site and put in all the proper codes. Finally, they had to market their results so that their site was heavily used.

Educators had just begun to speak about honoring different kinds of "intelligences"—verbal, visual, mathematical, emotional, musical, and kinesthetic.[7] ThinkQuest was ahead of its time in recognizing all these capabilities and encouraging students to draw on their unique gifts.

SCHOLARSHIP AWARDS

The contest was also an opportunity to win big and come away with enough award money to help pay for a college education. Every year, ThinkQuest gave away $1 million in scholarships and cash awards, with $25,000 going to every student on the team that produced the Best of Contest. Coaches and schools received $5,000 each.

First-place wins in five categories garnered $15,000 for every student, and $2,500 each to coaches and schools. Even those who came in fifth received some recognition: $3,000 for the students and $500 each to coaches and schools.

But ThinkQuest was about much more than award money. It provided role models for the next generation and introduced them to leaders in science, medicine, government, and the arts. News makers and celebrities presented the students with their trophies. Our first winners received awards from Gene Sperling, chief economic adviser to President Clinton; Ron Howard, film writer, producer, and director (*Splash* and *Apollo 13*); and Ken Wilson, a Nobel Laureate in physics and chemistry.

That first year, our emcee, the comedian Sinbad, learned that ThinkQuest kids were expert marketers, too. In the lab, one enterprising finalist had rigged up a flash screen with a subliminal message—"Sinbad, COME HERE!"—that also played the theme music from the entertainer's latest film, *Jingle All the Way*.

The following year, our presenters included Dr. Mary Harper, the first African American to graduate from the University of Minnesota and one of the original Tuskegee nurses; soccer superstar Mia Hamm; George Bednarz, Nobel recipient for his work on superconductivity; and Tim Berners-Lee, founder of the World Wide Web, who noted that ThinkQuest finalists had mastered the art of creating information networks.

REACHING OUT TO EDUCATORS

Introducing kids to computers was relatively straightforward, but getting the 70,000 independent educational systems in the United States to embrace technology was far more challenging. While schools with tech programs were eager to embrace ThinkQuest, others had no idea how to promote computer learning. A principal from Washington, D.C., for instance, was eager to participate in the ThinkQuest seminars the first year, but he couldn't afford to hire substitutes while his teachers were being trained. ANS picked up the tab, but we wondered how many other schools might have acquired computers but had no money allotted in their budget to instruct teachers how to use them.

We soon came up against another roadblock. The ThinkQuest contest didn't fit into school metrics, edu-talk for proving that kids were learning at a certain rate. Administrators had to prove the value of a problem and tie it to some concrete measure of academic performance. In the first year of the competition, I met the superintendent of schools near our headquarters in Armonk, New York, and asked him: "How can we get this program into your classrooms? What can we do to help?"

"You've got a great idea," he said, "but it isn't going to work for us."

"Why not?"

"I'm focusing on tests. If I lose a few points off the standard performance for my district," he explained, "I'll lose my job. That's where our attention has to go."

This administrator was not alone. Long before Congress authorized the "No Child Left Behind" program in 2001, schools had started teaching to the test. The companies that were producing educational software at that time followed suit.

In fall 1997, Roberts invited us to meet with leaders in educational technology. The government was about to launch a $2.25 billion program that would bring the Internet to all of our nation's schools and libraries. Once the schools were "Internet ready," Roberts envisioned computers as the first-line learning tool, with textbooks as the backup.

We tossed out some ideas for visually exciting software that would teach the basic concepts of chemistry and biology. The software executives didn't bite.

"We can't do this," they said. "We have to focus on the SATs and other tests. That's all the schools are buying." It was the same Catch-22 again. The school systems were locked into teaching to the test, and the only thing educational software companies could do was fall into line.

ThinkQuest was successful because it was subversive and spoke directly to the kids. It took a couple of years to prove to the educational establishment that students who learn to use the Internet fare better academically and make advances in all subjects. But the contest really took flight because it fostered a high level of engagement and promoted the students' own passions. Our finalists put in hundreds of hours on their ThinkQuest websites, working in the evenings, on weekends, and during summer vacations. When they finished their projects, they were especially proud of what they had built. They had discovered a direct line to their own creativity.

After just one year, the contest was so popular that students and their families were willing to fight for it. Though we planned our awards ceremony to coincide with school vacation, some districts were on different schedules. When finalists from Long Island were told they couldn't have two days off to attend our ceremony in Washington, D.C., their parents, who had put in countless hours of coaching, were furious. "How would this look in the local papers?" they said to the principal. "Shall we tell reporters that you kept our team from claiming their scholarships?" The school relented, and the team came to Washington to receive its awards. The school received a cash award as well.

Many school administrators began to give us their support at the end of 1997. There were three reasons for this new receptivity. First, there was a growing grassroots movement to promote online education. Through a California-based nonprofit called NetDay, for example, volunteers from business, education, and the community began to wire up local schools. Along with 20,000 others, President Clinton and Vice President Gore showed up wearing hard hats for the organization's first event.

The second reason administrators came on board was that ThinkQuest was hailed as a pioneer in project-based learning, and we received recognition from the educational community as a result. In fact, the CEO Forum on Education and Technology said our approach to online education was the wave of the future.[8]

And third, studies showed how the Internet helped boost academic performance. Policy makers called on the country's schools to start teaching creativity, cooperation, and critical thinking as the skills most needed in the digital age.

CREATING NEW EDUCATIONAL SOFTWARE

W. Edwards Deming said that innovation is driven by the producer, not the customer. Yet ThinkQuest turned this conventional wisdom on its head. In our program, the two were one and the same. The educational software industry created programs focused on rote testing; the most exciting programs were created by kids. The ThinkQuest library now included many popular teaching tools. A team from New York State produced *CHEMystery—Interactive Guide* that covered "everything high school students need to know about chemistry in a fun, imaginative, comprehensive manner." Teens from Delaware produced *Interactive Mathematics Online*, offering tutorials in algebra and trigonometry with bonus software thrown in for creating "stereograms," or three-dimensional optical illusions. The ThinkQuest library was fast becoming an educational theme park, a place where students struggling with a concept could go for extra help.

As Roberts said, "ThinkQuest students set the standard for online learning. The genius of this program was that it said to them, 'Come up with your best ideas about how to learn economics or math or history and put them on your websites.' In the mid-1990s, most of the computer materials used in schools were little more than drill and practice. Suddenly kids had a chance to develop programs for their peers that were both educational and fun."

By 1997, the ThinkQuest library was drawing more than 1 million hits a day. The following year, it was up to 20 million hits a week. The kids themselves had built the world's primary source for online education.

Advantages of a "Technology Pull"

ThinkQuest proved that you get more results with a "technology pull" than you do with a "technology push." There's a world of difference between the two.

In a technology push, you give equipment away, hoping to hook the user in. IBM did this in the 1970s, providing multimillion-dollar computers to universities that would then buy additional memory and service from the company. This strategy worked until the early

1990s, when technology changed and started appealing to a different audience. IBM gave high-powered PCs to the University of Texas, but no one knew what to do with them. *Pushing* technology on people doesn't work. Unless there is some obvious use for the hardware, it will sit around unused.

When we started ThinkQuest, our strategy was to *pull* the students and teachers in by showing them what they could accomplish with computers and the Internet. The $1 million we offered in awards and scholarships also got their attention. Over time, our students got so hooked on the new technology that they began to up the ante, using more sophisticated tools to construct their websites. They'd start to build a home page with html, and then they'd jazz it up with flash graphics and add music to make it more exciting. We also allowed ThinkQuest participants to update their content, post feedback from others, and add the latest trends in web design. As a result, they kept up with the latest software and equipment.

Many ThinkQuest teens became so expert that they started consulting in web development and running their own businesses. One of these enterprising students, Brent Lightner, sent us this note after he won a ThinkQuest award: "Hiya! You don't know me, but you changed my life."

As a senior in Hollidaysburg, Pennsylvania, Brent learned the Internet from the ground up in hopes of winning a college scholarship. Brent and his teammates turned to the arts, and they produced *The Interactive Music Emporium,* featuring a music generator that allowed users to compose using all of the orchestral instruments.

By the time he graduated, Brent was running a successful web design business, hiring fourteen-year-old hot shots to do the graphics. During an interview with the *Wall Street Journal,* Brent admitted that he was so busy, he'd gladly trade a website for a date.

He kept his web business going during his junior year abroad at the University of Leeds in England. "It sure beat flipping burgers to pay for college, and [I've] learned that I can run a web design business anywhere in the world."

His firm, TAOTI (which stands for The Art of the Internet), now has a wide range of clients including the World Bank, the California State Senate, and Penn State University. Brent's key lesson from ThinkQuest? "Don't hesitate to go after what you want. We go head to head with much larger companies to bid for contracts and aren't intimidated by the size and scale of any project."

CHAPTER 8

GOING GLOBAL

National borders aren't even speed bumps on the information superhighway.
Tim May

IN 1997, WE TOOK ThinkQuest international and began to tap the full collaborative power of the Internet. Hagen Hultzsch, a member of the board of Deutsche Telekom, worked with the German Federal Ministry for Education and Research to bring thirty-four thousand schools online with a program called *Schulen ans Netz* (schools on the Net). They quickly formed fifteen ThinkQuest teams with students from other countries. The Dutch national telephone company and Migros, a chain of Swiss food co-ops, also agreed to promote our contest. Singapore's Ministry of Education made ThinkQuest part of its standard curriculum overnight, producing fifteen finalists. The contest soon spread to India and Hong Kong.

Egyptian venture capitalist Hisham El Sherif set up computer shacks along the Nile, engaging young people who had never before set eyes on a computer. Excited by the chance for their children to win ThinkQuest scholarships, parents chipped in to buy memory upgrades and graphics cards.

The Internet Society gave us a global bully pulpit to talk about ThinkQuest, and every time we spoke at an international conference, we found new global partners. Soon ThinkQuest International was growing as fast as the World Wide Web. Within a year, fourteen ministries of education had adopted the contest; we sorely needed someone to manage our overseas operations.

When we first launched the competition, we hired a retiree named Grant Beglarian as a temp worker to help us distribute ThinkQuest packets to the schools. This elegant gray-haired gentleman was still with us two years later and was busily putting pushpins on a world map to show every country that had a ThinkQuest team. One of our summer interns alerted us to Beglarian's resume. "Did you know that Beglarian is a well-known composer and was president of the National Foundation for Advancement in the Arts? He also speaks eight languages."

We immediately asked Beglarian, "Why are you working here for only $10 an hour?"

"I've just retired," he said. "This is a wonderful program, and I'd like to help."

"Then why don't you run our international program from now on?"

Beglarian was the perfect ambassador. Witty and urbane, he put our foreign partners at ease. Born in Russia, Beglarian had come to the United States to study with Aaron Copland. Under Leonard Bernstein, the New York Philharmonic had performed Beglarian's orchestral suites, and he was familiar with the cultural capitals of Europe, Asia, and the Middle East. In his second career, Beglarian helped our international partners work in harmony, setting up their own online libraries and feeder contests.

GLOBAL THEMES

In 1997, Best of Contest went to a team spread across three continents. Participants from India, the Netherlands, and the United States created *Himalayas: Where Earth Meets Sky*, which explores this legendary mountain range, describing recent environmental problems caused by earthquakes and erosion and producing the most comprehensive website on this subject on the Internet.

During the course of the contest, two members of the team relocated: Debangsu Sengupta moved from India to the Ivory Coast, while Yian Chen moved from the United States to Taiwan. "Thanks to the presence and stability of the Internet," the team reported, "we were able to stay in touch with each other and carry on with our project." Our first international winners were a perfect illustration of the benefits of online collaboration.

A team from Australia, India, and the United States took on the problem of a rapidly aging world population, looking ahead to the turn of the century. *Link-Age 2000* opened with a population counter, noting every second the increase in the number of people over sixty-five—the total in September 1977 was well past the 500 million mark. This site challenged users to overcome their prejudices about aging—*crone decrepit doddering elderly feeble frail old bag old dog old geezer old goat*—and urged students to consider careers in gerontology. It also contained a game called "Sim Age 2000" that examined the importance of a graying population. "Students act as the mayor of a fictional town in which policy decisions, the state of the economy, and scientific research all contribute to the size and quality of life of a population."

DRAWING LARGER AUDIENCES

By September 1977, our students were pretty savvy about product development. They were choosing subjects that they knew would get a lot of hits and reaching wider audiences with the aid of marketing and publicity. Every ThinkQuest entry had to scale, meaning that it had to work on all platforms and browsers and be accessible to a large number of users.

A BROADER AUDIENCE AT HOME

As ThinkQuest spread abroad, we also made an effort to reach students in the isolated areas of the United States. Alex Kulezsca, a teen from a Washington, D.C., suburb, teamed up with Granite Christopher, a student from Alaska's Kenai peninsula, to produce a website on the mysteries of sound.

Email was the only way Alex could consult with Granite. "This was a huge disadvantage when it came to brainstorming," said Alex, "but it forced us to be organized in our approach, and to clearly define our tasks before we set to work." Midway through the contest, Granite took off on a family fishing trip, hoping to catch enough food to survive the long Alaskan winter. It would be a dangerous journey on icy seas. "If we're lucky," he emailed, "we'll be back in a week."

"Despite his elemental lifestyle, Granite was technologically sophisticated," Alex said. "He had the answers to many of our software questions. When we finally met at the awards ceremony, he taught me to use one of the first digital cameras that recorded onto floppy disks."

Helping Kids with Disabilities

In the United States, educators used ThinkQuest to engage students who missed school because of health problems. For instance, the computer allowed Emilie Sutterlin, who suffers from chronic fatigue and chemical sensitivities, to explore her interest in math and science and work at her own pace. After interviewing experts at the National Institutes of Health, Emilie produced a website on sleep disorders and related illnesses.

The next year, she teamed up with Swiss student Michael Muelly and began to learn about human memory. Her entry explained Alzheimer's disease and showed how memories are heightened during war and trauma. It also evaluated computer memory, asking how close machines can get to human recollection. Through ThinkQuest, Emilie interviewed and corresponded with many of the nation's top researchers. She is attending Penn State College of Medicine and plans to specialize in neuropsychiatry.

(Note: I personally stay in touch with many of the ThinkQuesters. They send me letters from time to time, and sometimes I cry from happiness. I consider myself so very lucky to have been able to provide this opportunity for these creative young students.)

First place in the arts and literature category that year went to a team from New York, New Jersey, and Texas, for a topic with wide appeal—*The Motion Picture Industry: Behind-the-Scenes*. This site attracted the budding filmmaker in everyone, providing a simulation that allowed students to

- Work with a screenwriter to create a script;
- Cast the actors they felt would be best for the different roles;
- Choose how to frame the shots;
- Add sound effects; and
- Choose what kind of advertising campaign they wanted for publicity for their film.

The team drove home the importance of having a good business plan. "Be careful!" they warned. "You have to stay under the given budget and you have to produce a good film, or else you could be dealing with a major financial loss as well as a bad reputation." To draw industry attention to their site, the students invited one hundred well-known directors and producers to create the world's first online movie.

As ThinkQuest websites reached larger audiences, however, they grew more expensive to operate. For example, David Leung, from San Diego, created *Investing in Your Future*, a website that explained the role of brokerage houses, mutual funds, gold, CDs, and 401Ks. Teaming up with two other California teens, he later created *Invest Smart*, the most popular website on the ThinkQuest server for several years. With more than a million hits a day, this site cost ANS in excess of $100,000 annually in maintenance fees.

WHAT IF WE MISSED A GEM?

We were worried in 1997 that we might have a few "sleepers" among our entries—websites that would prove useful over time and capture audiences we never dreamed of. So we began to look at the usage of all our entries, including websites from previous years that had failed to win an award. A simple entry on American sign language popped up as one of the most broadly used educational resources. We had overlooked it because it had such primitive graphics, yet this turned out to be a plus. This basic teaching aid ran on the most basic computers and the lowest-speed telephone lines, and its very lack of sophistication made it accessible to a wide audience. *SignHEAR* was reaching people of all ages and income levels all over the world, so it took our first-ever "Gem Award."

THINKQUEST KIDS BECOME THE NEW CELEBRITIES

As the contest grew, our winners were profiled in *People* magazine and the *Wall Street Journal*. By now, they were experts at handling the media. And upon returning home, many received a hero's welcome from their schools and communities. But perhaps the ultimate compliment came during our awards ceremony in 1997.

When we convened in Washington, D.C., we shared a hotel with the San Francisco 49ers, who were slated to play the Washington Redskins. Though they were surrounded by candidates for football's Hall of Fame, most of our kids were unfazed: Many came from far-flung countries and didn't follow American sports. The world-class wide receiver Jerry Rice, however, was intrigued by so many teens with laptops chattering away in different languages. He asked Carol Calderwood, one of our ThinkQuest coaches, "Who are all these kids?"

As she described our educational Olympics on the Internet, Rice turned to his teammates and said, "Hey, guys, do you realize we've been riding in the elevator with a bunch of geniuses?"

SHOWING WHAT A SINGLE SCHOOL CAN DO

Don Hyatt's computer lab at Thomas Jefferson High in Alexandria, Virginia, produced a record number of finalists in 1997, showing what a single school can do. Among their entries were:

Chess Dominion, an interactive tutorial designed by two chess masters under the age of seventeen: Charles Gelman and his opponent at a then-recent tournament, Jennie Frenklakh, from Belarus. Their home page opened with an ancient Indian proverb, "Chess is a sea in which a mosquito can bathe and an elephant can drown." The students added their own brand of humor, showing a bishop gliding on a surfboard, and introducing Deep Blue, the chess-playing IBM computer that beat grandmaster Gary Kasparov that year.

Baseball: The Game and Beyond, in which two varsity athletes give an inside tour of their sport. Joe Giuliani (a nephew of the former New York City mayor) and Ken Conley provided vintage commentary from the announcer's booth, showed what goes on in the bullpen, then explained why a curve ball curves and how a player's "earned run average" is calculated.

You Are What You Eat, a personalized site for weight management produced by Brent Metz, a typical American teenager living on Starbursts and Jolt Cola, and two teammates from Russia. Students entered their age, height, and weight, and then found out how many calories they needed each day and what foods would provide them with the most nutrition. Brent later expanded this website, adding a speech recognition component. "You simply talked to the computer and told it what you ate that day," he said. It then told users how much weight they'd gain after indulging in a burger and fries.

Holocaust, a website that included audio clips from concentration camp survivors. When local schoolchildren laughed at the movie *Schindler's List*, not realizing that it was based on actual events, Jordan Feil and his team decided to focus on the plight of Jews in Nazi Germany. They also reported on the Nuremberg trials and the victims' efforts to retrieve their assets from Swiss bank accounts. A stark time line shows the proliferation of the camps alongside a strip of barbed wire.

Hyatt's computer lab took top honors that year, along with two websites submitted by other contestants that provided a three-dimensional re-creation of Shakespeare's Globe Theatre and a virtual tour of the human body.

CHAPTER 9

REACHING
AT-RISK KIDS

Education isn't preparation for life. It's life itself.

John Dewey

THE TERM *AT RISK* REFERS TO TEENS from low-income families who are likely to drop out of school. In its early years, ThinkQuest proved that computer education could make a difference and keep these kids engaged.

Our first success story involved three students from Perry Middle School in Miramar, Florida. As the semester began, two of them in particular, Steve and Xavier, were hard to manage. They couldn't sit still, and they constantly made fun of each other in class. But their teacher, Judy Shasek, found a novel way to engage the two adolescents. First she taught them juggling, and then she entered them in ThinkQuest.

"Juggling improved their concentration and got them working as a team," said Shasek. "They started with an exercise that emphasized cooperation. One kid would toss the ball into the air, but another kid would have to catch it. This wasn't easy. But with practice, the kids began to focus and coordinate their efforts."

By adding or taking away objects from this exercise, Shasek could teach some basic math. "Having a concrete physical task made all the difference for these kids," she said. "The more physically active they were, the more likely they were to learn."

There was already some solid evidence from researchers indicating that exercise boosts learning and retention. Yet Shasek felt that it might boost self-esteem as well. To test her theory, she asked her teens to give a demonstration at the local grade school.

"How many eggs do we need to make muffins?" the jugglers asked as the grade-schoolers looked on with glee. "They'd toss some eggs into the air and some would break. Then the whole class would howl with laughter—third graders had no idea math could be so much fun," Shasek told us. "Yet this was a real turning point for the older boys . . . They learned how to manage a group and talk to an audience. They were no longer the dumb ones who required special tutoring. Suddenly they had an expertise that they could share with others."

Steve and Xavier were both pegged as too slow to handle academic work. Yet their grades improved as they participated in the juggling project, and they made exceptional progress. "A whole new world opened up to them after they went to the Barnum and Bailey circus and encountered a Russian girl who could juggle 16 objects lying down," says Shasek. "They learned that they could learn new skills if they put their minds to it." The boys then started to work with hoops and pins. Within weeks their concentration and grades improved. Next they decided to enter ThinkQuest and master some computer skills.

The team didn't win an award, but their website, *Juggling It All*, brought their work to a much larger audience. ANS sent a documentary film crew to record their performances and screened it at the ThinkQuest awards event as proof that no matter what their starting point, young people have the power to change their lives. And that everyone who participates in ThinkQuest is a winner.

DISCOVERING TECHNOLOGY

Like many teachers in the late 1990s did, Shasek discovered computers through "a happy accident." As a part-time science instructor, her main job was writing grant applications. The school provided her with a computer, and it was such a novelty that students gathered around it on their lunch hour. After a few days, they started to experiment with the machine.

When Shasek turned her computer on one morning, her picture popped up on the screen. So she asked the kids to show her what other features they had mastered. Two months later, they had convinced her to buy animation and game software and to write a grant for a computer lab.

"Some of these kids had juvenile records and weren't doing so well in school," Shasek said. "So we made a deal. They had to complete their school assignments before they could play around on the new equipment. These students formed a group called Network Navigators and started helping teachers integrate technology into the curriculum. Then they started doing ThinkQuest, and computers became the new vocational technology."

Ivan, a sixth grader, routinely cut language arts because he was terrified of words. "Somehow he found his way into my computer class and began using animation," said Shasek. "He would write ten pages a night describing his scenarios, but he couldn't spell, so I teamed him up with a shy girl who was good with language, who would type his stories. Together, they discovered new creative worlds."

By 1998, mainstream educators had discovered a strong link between computer education and better writing skills.[9] Researchers at the University of Michigan noted that computers could help students become better communicators in all media, yet, they warned, students can get so engrossed in the computer, they forget about the teacher![10]

On yet another issue, Shasek was ahead of the curve. Instinctively, she was using movement and exercise to ground her students. The next year, her ThinkQuest team made the finals. At our awards ceremony, she was pleased to find out that we had set up rumpus rooms where kids could rock climb, joust in padded garments, and play a variety of aerobic games. Like Shasek, we believed it was important to keep kids anchored in the physical world as they ventured into cyberspace.

This gifted teacher was among the first to help at-risk kids with a program combining physical activity and computers. She later went on to found generationfit.com, an organization that uses exercise to boost the learning process.

CHAPTER 10

A TEEN UNITED NATIONS

The Internet is becoming the town square for the global village of tomorrow.

Bill Gates

IN 1998, THE THINKQUEST annual awards ceremony looked like a youthful version of the United Nations. We had nearly six thousand teams from seventy-five countries, and 38 percent of our students were from outside the United States. As a result, ThinkQuest participants were now learning as much about other cultures as they were about technology and content.

ANOTHER INTERNET "FIRST"

To help students find teammates in other countries, we set up the first "matchmaking" service on the Web. We also created chat rooms, newsgroups, and email accounts to facilitate online collaboration. A frequent chat room sign-off, "Good morning, good afternoon, and good night!" indicated that students were now collaborating across different time zones.

Paris Treantafeles, a techie who created light shows for rock concerts, was our mentor-in-chief, and he ran the help desk. Elfin and energetic, Treantafeles had an easy rapport with the ThinkQuest kids who routinely turned to him for help with last-minute bugs. Like most teens, they were masters of procrastination. Thousands of teams waited until the final week of the contest to download their websites. Treantafeles slept on the floor of his office and was online 24/7 answering panicked emails about lost web pages and video links.

For example, one team discovered a technical snag just minutes after the server closed. Entranced by the drawings of M. C. Escher, Alok Bushan and his fellow students created a website called *Totally Tessellated,* exploring patterns made by interlocking shapes. The directions to enter the site appeared in such a small font, the students wondered if users would see it. The judges were able to navigate the site and liked what they saw. *Totally Tessellated* won an award for its animated graphics, and the students learned to test their work well in advance—on every browser.

CLICK HERE TO READ THIS SITE IN ENGLISH, CHINESE, HINDI . . .

Bilingual websites were now the rage. As ThinkQuest went international, even students in remote countries began to create entries in English as well as in their native tongue. "Nowadays, anyone who cannot speak English and is incapable of using the Internet is regarded as backward," said the philanthropist Al-Waleed bin Talal, called "The Arabian Warren Buffett" by *Fortune* magazine.

In 1999, ThinkQuest saw its greatest growth outside the United States. Within a year of our going global, 51 percent of our entrants hailed from eighty countries. To make the ThinkQuest website safe for student use, we had to check any interactive postings for profanity—in several languages—and the appropriateness of the added

IMPROVING INFORMATION LITERACY

Students from around the world enlightened one another with their views of the news and web media. It reminds me of the story of the blind men and the elephant:

> Three blind men encounter an elephant.
>
> The first man touches the elephant's tail and says, "It's exactly like a rope."
>
> The second man bumps into the side of the elephant and says, "It is like a wall."
>
> Then the third man grabs the elephant's trunk and says, "You are all wrong; the elephant is just like a snake."

Just as the blind men learned from one another's observations, the students learned and taught one another that any information has multiple sides. We call this *information literacy*. They learned that when they surf the Web for a topic of interest, it is critical to look at many sources—all the sides—and then from their analysis of multiple sources of information they can draw their own conclusions. As students built their websites and filtered the information they would use to teach others, they became information literate.

Information literacy emerged as an important theme in 1998 as international teams grappled with the escalating violent conflicts worldwide, from Kosovo to the Middle East. One team compared news reports in the *Washington Post* with articles in Israeli, Arabic, and Asian newspapers, asking, "When you read the same story from several different viewpoints, how do you tell which one is right?"

Other students also used their websites to explore topics that had been neglected or were considered controversial by the general press. For instance, a team from Hawaii and Sweden was intrigued by the multiple roles television plays in our time: as a source of news, as entertainment, and as a means of selling everything from deodorant to cars. They produced *Electric Snow*, a website that also explained the V-chip that allows parents to control what programs their children watch on TV.

Students from the United States, Norway, and China launched the *Global Gazette*, an online paper providing information about traditions, sports, governments, arts and music, norms, and everyday life on three continents. This site won the ThinkQuest collaboration award for team diversity.

An international team parsed the recent headlines about global warming. *Energy Matters* offered a guide to alternative energy sources such as fossil fuels—coal, wood, oil, and natural gas—nuclear energy, and solar, wind, and geothermal power. The site also provided a computer simulation that invited students to solve the energy crisis.

Singapore's Galvin Sng worked with American and Dutch teammates to produce *Volcanoes Online*, a site describing the shifting of Earth's plates and the state of the world's most famous volcanoes. This dual-language website (English and Dutch) included a "Volcano" comic strip and a game called "Save the Village" that focused on disaster preparedness. "Every correct answer saves 800 people!" the site proclaimed.

Former three-time winner of ThinkQuest from 1996 through 1998, the Californian Kushal Dave worked with students from Australia and the Netherlands to create *Death: An Inquiry into Man's Immortality*, bravely taking on a subject that was then considered taboo by the American media. The students considered the leading causes of death in various countries; explored how hospice workers, filmmakers, poets, and artists view the dying process; and summarized different spiritual beliefs about the afterlife.

(Kushal graduated from Yale and was instrumental in designing Google Notebook. His weekly blog covers everything from food and travel to technology reviews and media literacy. For example, "Forty-five percent of Americans say they believe little or nothing of what they read in their daily newspapers. *Actual study. Sigh.*")

After reading about Dolly, the first cloned sheep, students from Round Rock, Texas, investigated the biological and ethical aspects of cloning, surveying people in several countries about the moral and medical issues raised by such experiments.

---

images. As our international participation skyrocketed, we began to adapt our contest rules to local needs. Students in the Netherlands, for example, went to university tuition free, so we allowed them to use their ThinkQuest awards to pay for housing instead. The Japanese government wanted to get families involved in computer education, so we encouraged parents to serve as coaches. But the question we were most eager to explore with each one of our national partners was how ThinkQuest might improve their students' quality of life.

When we met with officials at Singapore's Ministry of Education, we said, "You have the top test scores in the world in math and science. Your kids are incredibly competitive. But what are they are missing?"

A chorus of voices replied, "Their youth!"

The minister then suggested that we modify our judging to reward websites that made learning more fun. We did so, and Think-Quest grew like wildfire in this country because kids suddenly saw the contest as play, not work. It gave them a chance to express their passion and their individuality with no holds barred. As the novelist Tom Robbins said, "Humanity has advanced . . . not because it has been sober, responsible, and cautious, but because it has been playful, rebellious, and immature."

AN UNEXPECTED HERO

As ThinkQuest grew, we began to bridge the digital divide in developing countries. Sizwe, an artist from the African bush, was learning disabled, plus he had no computer. Yet neither obstacle stopped him from entering the contest. How? A team of Singaporean students assembled a thumbnail history of the twentieth century, covering a hundred years of events and trends in politics, media, transportation, science, art, and the environment. Then Sizwe illustrated each web page, producing time lines and "state of the world" maps. Sizwe's teacher scanned his imaginative designs onto a CD, then drove through the bush to an Internet café and emailed them to his teammates.

When *The Passing of a Century* made the ThinkQuest finals, we contacted the South African consulate to obtain a visa so Sizwe could attend our awards ceremony in Los Angeles.

"You must have the wrong student," the official said. "This young man couldn't possibly have entered an international compe-

TRAINING TOMORROW'S LEADERS

A recent poll revealed that many of our early winners are now CEOs of their own start-up companies or rising stars at industry giants like Microsoft and Google. Others are giving back to their communities as computer mentors. The following list of snapshots shows how ThinkQuest winners have fared in the early stage of their careers:

Australian Ashleigh Green got hooked into ThinkQuest after his mother served as a coach for the contest's award-winning site *Shakespeare's Globe Theatre* in 1997. In 1998, Ashleigh and his team created *True Values*, exploring the work of environmentalist John Walmsley, the first writer to assign monetary values to the functions of the natural world.

After graduating from college, Ashleigh created a start-up company called Platypus Software. It's now a Microsoft Gold Certified Partner specializing in content management as well as networking and related products.

Fellow Aussie Alice Whittington partnered with Ashleigh on *True Values*, and then went on to pursue two degrees: one in business and one in languages. She became fluent in German and French while studying abroad at two European universities. Now based in London, Alice runs international corporate events for ultra-high-net-worth private clients at Barclays Bank. She hopes one day to help clients invest their wealth in socially responsible projects.

"Our generation was in danger of becoming complacent," she says. "Yet ThinkQuest showed us how to push past that and think about technology and the environment and ways to create better standards of living around the world."

Manas Mittal's ThinkQuest scholarship allowed him to purchase a laptop and led him to attend graduate school in engineering. Today, he works at MIT's media laboratory on sensor networks and the visualizing of sensor data. "One of our projects I've been working on is to build a real-life tricorder like the one you've seen on *Star Trek*. Once you point this device in a certain direction, you will be able to browse sensor data and see beyond what is immediately visible to the naked eye."

Mohamed El-Zohairy, who with teammates from Australia and the United States created *Blood—The River of Life* in 2001, grew up in a working-class family in Egypt and went to a crowded public school. "There were barely any functional science labs, let alone computer labs," he recalls. "I fell in love with computer science when I was in sixth grade but was only able to afford a computer in the tenth grade, a year before entering ThinkQuest."

Mohamed later served as a coach for other ThinkQuest teams in Egypt and Africa, and he received the only full scholarship available to Egyptian students to attend an American university. He now works as a project manager at a software engineering company.

Keiji Oenoki, who created *Physics Today* in 1997 with his team from Peru, received his BA in computer science in 2000 and is now a software design engineer at Microsoft. "Though the state of the art in web development is vastly different now," Keiji says, "ThinkQuest gave me a technical foundation from which to learn new web standards and technologies. It also taught me how to work with other people. An ability to communicate and collaborate is as important as the ability to write good code."

India's Debangsu Sengupta—together with teammates Vikas Sonak, from the Netherlands, and Woodbridge Green, from the United States— took Best of Contest in 1997 for *Himalayas: Where Earth Meets Sky*. The following year, Debangsu and his team received second place for *Living Africa*. After working for four years as a software engineer at Microsoft, he enrolled at Stanford University to earn a graduate degree in computer science. "ThinkQuest was at the cutting edge," says Debangsu. "A lot of the issues we worked through—dealing with different languages, cultures, time zones, schedules, and global coordination—are important in organizations today. The competition also received widespread coverage in India and set the stage for the outsourcing boom in my country."

With his teammates, Steve Kessler created a website on computers for ThinkQuest 1998, and then he took second place for *The Art of Speech* in the year 2000. After college, he set up his own data management company, Denver Data Man. "My ThinkQuest experience influences everything I do," he says. "It taught me project management, research, and communication skills. For *The Art of Speech,* I managed the team over three time zones and produced over three hundred pages of content. And I helped develop systems for content control that are still useful today." Steve currently works for KidsTek (www.kidstek.org) teaching at-risk kids how to use computers.

Chris Glazner went from being a computer novice to earning an MIT doctorate in engineering by way of two ThinkQuest scholarships—for *Southern PowWows* (1996) and *Trumpeter's Fanfare* (1997). Chris's project on Native Americans has been quoted on Wikipedia. "We got a huge kick out of the fact that they cited a couple of sixteen-year-olds," he said. He is now doing research in systems architecture for the federal government.

Josh Tauberer is a fifth-year doctoral student at the University of Pennsylvania in the linguistics program. His primary academic interest is phonetics and computational models of grammar acquisition. He has also been using government data to improve civic education. In his spare time, he runs Gov-Track.us, a noncommercial and nonpartisan tool that helps people research and track the activities of the U.S. Congress. The site has roughly ten thousand visitors a day, and it has contributed to the federal government's transparency. The idea for GovTrack came to Josh when he was trying to decide on a new web project after his team's ThinkQuest entry, *Webcytology: An Exploration of Unicellular Life*, received the second-place award in 1999.

tition. He doesn't have the resources." The U.S. State Department intervened on our behalf, and Sizwe, who had never left his village, crossed an ocean to receive his scholarship. The real payoff, however, was the hero's welcome he received upon his return. Sizwe's teachers took him around to other villages, telling students, "If he can do it, so can you."

A PATH TO ECONOMIC INDEPENDENCE

One of our goals was to introduce students to the economic potential of the Internet. The kids themselves created the best tutorial on this topic, showing their peers how to set up online businesses. "There were no resources for people my age," said team leader Melissa Sconyers, "and a lot of teens were interested in e-business. All you need is a good idea. On the Internet, no one knows if you're a kid."

In middle school, Melissa joined the ranks of the homeschooled and designed her own independent study program. Working with teammates was a challenge since Melissa was used to learning on her own. Yet once the group agreed on a design for the website, things went smoothly. Melissa wrote the code and, with her teammates from Texas and Jamaica, produced fifty pages of original content.

Ebiz4teens offered a wide range of information to budding entrepreneurs: This included tutorials on creating dynamic business plans, writing professional resumes, and negotiating contracts. It also provided links to technology-related business organizations in several countries. The biggest draw was a series of "success stories" showing how teen entrepreneurs had created viable online businesses. The website was eventually translated into eight languages.

After their ThinkQuest win, the Ebiz team spent a summer in Jamaica, teaching Internet skills to students aged ten to eighteen. "We'd show one kid how to code a website and he'd go out and teach five more," Melissa said. "It spread like a virus."

Melissa worked as a web designer all through college. After an additional year of studying Chinese in Beijing, Melissa landed a position with the Chinese government to consult on web traffic related to the 2008 Olympics. She has since been featured on Oprah's special on "Smart Kids," and in the *New York Times,* the *Wall Street Journal, Wired, Cosmo Girl,* and *BusinessWeek.*

MOVING TO HOLLYWOOD

In 1999, we moved our awards ceremonies to Los Angeles, where we gave the students and their coaches a tour of Universal Studios and introduced them to headliners in the entertainment industry. Through writer, director, and producer Jim Brooks, for example, they met the actors from the TV series *The Simpsons.* Our emcee was Leonard Nimoy, "Mr. Spock" on the original *Star Trek.* Richard Riordan, the mayor of Los Angeles, gave ThinkQuest the key to the city and noted that ThinkQuest was the largest and fastest-growing Internet-based educational program in the world.

We received other accolades as well. That year, the American Library Association said our student websites were among the nation's finest teaching tools. ThinkQuest was now considered the most comprehensive educational resource on the web. And we had proven that students do their best work when they are allowed to work on independent projects. As Albert Einstein once observed: "Imagination is more important than knowledge. For while knowledge defines all we currently know and understand, imagination points to all we might yet discover and create."

CHAPTER 11

LAUNCHING THINKQUEST JUNIOR

The whole art of teaching is the art of awakening the natural curiosity of young minds in order to satisfy them later on.

Anatole France

AFTER HEARING FIRST LADY HILLARY CLINTON talk about the importance of early childhood education at a conference in Los Angeles, I began thinking about ways to awaken the creativity of younger students. ThinkQuest was teaching teenagers how to problem solve and create new learning tools. Why not start these processes a few years earlier? Technology could help elementary schoolchildren explore the world on many levels. Computers were the new "mixed media," incorporating music, storytelling, visuals, and multilevel content in a single place. Structuring something where kids could work in larger teams in the classroom was easy, and we now had enough support from the schools to make this work.

By 1998, American educators were more receptive to technology. The percentage of U.S. public schools with Internet access had more than tripled, from 20 percent to 72 percent.[11] Our schools were now spending an average of $31 per student on computer services; this was a good time to take our contest into the early grades. On the red-eye flight from Los Angeles to New York, I outlined a program called ThinkQuest Junior that would target grades four through six and presented that program to the board the following morning.

"If you've ever watched eight-year-olds playing Nintendo," I said, "you know you'll never match their hand-eye coordination, their reaction time, their concentration, and their ability to think on so many different levels. In these early years, kids develop an intuitive understanding of technology. From then on, it's like an extension of their bodies. I think it's time we had a program just for them."

A PROGRAM OF THEIR OWN

We knew two things at the start. We couldn't expect fifth graders to work with teammates from other countries and deal with different time zones. It would be logistically impossible to bring grade-schoolers to a national awards ceremony. As a result, we decided to keep the program national and announce our winners online. Our awards would be scaled down as well. Instead of college scholarships, we would give laptops to the winning teams. Since website building required a wide range of skills, we increased the number of students on a team from three to six. We also revised the wording on our posters, saying "This contest is for *girls and boys* grades four through six," to work toward gender balance.

When we announced the contest, we didn't expect sophisticated entries. Yet the websites were both interesting and technically proficient, and it was clear that once these kids reached high school, they would take computer learning to a whole new level. Many of our international partners were so impressed by our first entries that they decided to run a version of ThinkQuest Junior on their own.

Our first year, Best of Contest went to a website about the rescue and release of a baby whale in Marina Del Rey, California. Other winning sites explored the Arctic Circle, Chinese calligraphy, ancient Egypt, and snowboarding. A team from Kenai, Alaska, told the story of the first Iditarod in 1925, when dogsleds carrying medicine raced through better than 650 miles of rough terrain to stem an outbreak of diphtheria. Some of the topics explored by other teams included multiplication (using Lego bricks to present the content), the origins of creativity, and how Down syndrome affected a classmate.

Our younger students made history come alive as well, interviewing their grandparents and great-grandparents about their experiences in World War II. "We learned about Guadalcanal, what it was like on a destroyer, food rationing, and much more," this team wrote on their home page. "We invite you to read our stories, then find out how World War II affected your family. Add your story to our website by clicking on the 'Tell Us Your Story' link below."

With very little promotion, more than five hundred teams signed up. Our entries doubled in the next academic year. In 1999, a study of ZIP codes showed that we were reaching schools across a broad socioeconomic range, and a survey of teachers showed that the contest made it easier to bring technology into the classroom. Nearly 90 percent of those teachers had recommended ThinkQuest to colleagues or students. Further, well over half of our ThinkQuest Junior entrants were now female. We had passed a watershed, eliminating gender boundaries in computer education.

ThinkQuest International and ThinkQuest Junior received many awards, including the coveted Global Information Infrastructure Award and the Deutsche Telekom and *Focus Magazine*'s Award for Education. These helped give us added credibility with educators and school administrators. In early 2000, Secretary of Education Richard Riley emphasized student-centered learning, multisensory stimulation, collaboration, the use of multimedia, and teaching in a "real world" context.[12]

Just as we had hoped, the contest was a catalyst for schools that had recently purchased computers but had no idea what to do with them. John Payne, a former technology executive who was teaching grade school in Tennessee, told us, "Although millions had been spent on hardware, [our] computers had become $2,500 Nintendo machines and overpriced typewriters." Payne entered his class in ThinkQuest Junior, telling them they would have to create educational websites on their own, with only minor help.

His fifth graders produced a website called *The Real Truth about Fast Food and Nutrition.* "They had to work hard to explain all the chemical compounds contained in processed foods in a way that could be understood by their peers," Payne said, "and the team was astonished to learn they'd reached the finals."

The students were fascinated by the other ThinkQuest entries. "I never saw so much enthusiasm for topics that were always considered BOR-ING! in the classroom," Payne recalled. One boy yelled out, "These kids are wrong about the Boston Massacre! They said only three people were killed."

Payne's class contacted the other ThinkQuest team, explaining that five colonists had been shot to death in March 1770 after taunting British soldiers. They cited their sources, and the other team emailed back, thanking them for the correction. Said Payne, "ThinkQuest taught students to value their own research and expertise."

After Payne's students received a first-place award for *The Real Truth about Fast Food and Nutrition,* the website was picked up by health classes in Australia and then by a Michigan nurse who was teaching patients about the basics of nutrition. To their great surprise, ThinkQuest Junior kids were teaching adults as well as their peers.

PS 56 TAKES THE LEAD

In 1999, a ThinkQuest Junior coach got a team in just under the wire. Neme Alperstein, a fifth-grade teacher from PS 56 in Queens (one of New York City's five boroughs), learned about the contest just ten minutes before our registration deadline. "I chose four kids at random, then told them they'd been entered in a web-building contest," she confessed. "One girl got so excited that she produced a guide to the Internet and taught the other kids how to write code. I didn't know a thing about creating websites, so she taught me as well."

Alperstein's students made the finals the first time out of the gate, and for the next eight years, they set the standard for the ThinkQuest Junior competition. We visited PS 56 to find out how this teacher managed to coach so many winning teams.

"Kids don't like to do what they're told to do," she explained. "But this contest made students come up with their own topics of study. All I had to do was encourage them and keep reminding them they were in charge." Alperstein asked parents to sign off on their children's ThinkQuest topics, and then she got stern with the kids. "You can't bail," she told them. "If you do, you're going to fail."

These students weren't intimidated in the least. PS 56 is one of New York City's schools for the gifted and talented. Students hail from China, Mexico, Russia, India, and Pakistan, and many see ThinkQuest Junior as a stepping-stone to academic achievement.

One of Alperstein's first ThinkQuest Junior students, Madelaine Gesslein, was worried about getting her teeth straightened, so she put a team together and decided to call her website *Yo, It's Time for Braces.*

"How come you picked that title?" Alperstein asked, concerned about the use of slang.

But the kids weren't trying to talk like boys from the 'hood. They were trying to outfox the system. Yo-yos were very popular at the time, and the kids discovered that any website with the keyword *yo* in it got picked up by search engines. Said Alperstein, "If you want to learn about Internet marketing, ask a devious child!"

Madelaine worked with two Russian immigrants, Svetlana and Valentine, to prepare a survey of orthodontists and then mailed it to a national institute. "The kids knew they had to do a good job because the experts would be watching," said Alperstein. After the website was posted, Hillary Clinton, Al Gore, and Rudolph Giuliani signed the guest book, and the site was translated into Chinese.

Since ThinkQuest Junior encouraged students to promote their sites, the braces team applied for a Global Information Infrastructure (GII) award. The GII honored contributions by industry to online learning, and when the kids realized they would be competing with the Mayo Clinic and the Library of Congress, they withdrew their application. "We don't belong in this category," they told the organizers. "We're only in fifth grade." The GII encouraged them to complete their entry form. Three months later, the team of three fifth graders was asked to accept an award at the GII ceremony in San Francisco.

"All the contestants were wearing black and had Bluetooth headsets," Alperstein recalls. "Paula Poundstone and South Park were the entertainment, and guests included Milton Chen, of the George Lucas Educational Foundation, and a Who's Who of corporate America. Valentine had to stand on a milk carton to reach the microphone, but at least he thought to bring a tux."

The ThinkQuest Junior team was profiled in the press, and soon the word was out: Contest entries translate into award money and trips to national conventions.

"I didn't have to sell this program anymore," Alperstein told us. "Parents couldn't sign their kids up fast enough."

The following year, Madelaine started collecting Pokemon cards and had, inadvertently, bought some fake ones with her birthday money. When she realized she'd been cheated, she put together a website called Art Rights and Wrongs: From Pokemon to Picasso. The site investigated copyright infringement, from counterfeit trading cards to art fakes, and interviewed experts from the Library of Congress.

For *Growing Up with Epilepsy*, fifth grader Alyssa Genna posted diary entries describing her seizures and explaining why epilepsy made her feel like an outsider. Her team also provided information on the latest clinical trials concerning the disease, and they interviewed experts at Columbia Presbyterian Hospital.

Andrew Polyak gained new confidence as he participated in the competition. Andrew was a natural with computers, but he was also shy. After completing his ThinkQuest Junior project, *Aviation in Viet Nam*, he became more outgoing and turned into the class technology mentor. But most important, he grew closer to his father, who had served as a mechanic on an aircraft carrier throughout the war. "Mr. Polyak did the repairs for every plane that took off, and he felt the pilots' lives were in his hands," says Alperstein. "This was the first time he talked about his experience. The project resulted in a stronger bond between father and son."

THE CONTEST THAT KEEPS ON GIVING

ThinkQuest Junior helped many students at PS 56 secure scholarships to the prep schools and colleges of their choice—even if they didn't reach the finals.

One team explored string theory, interviewing Michio Kaku, the world's leading expert on the topic. They had terrific content, but no flash graphics, so they didn't take an award. Still, their entry impressed Prep for Prep, a program that provides scholarships for minority students with intellectual promise. Each team member is now at a private school in Manhattan and headed for an Ivy League college.

The same was true for a team that explored nanotechnology. Eddie Bauer was using a process to make clothing that wouldn't stain, and students decided to find out how it worked. They talked to experts at Lawrence Livermore and other major research labs, but their website was eliminated in the final round of judging. Still, the content was so intriguing that the students were asked to speak at the National Educational Computing Conference. After this event, each one received a prep school scholarship. "ThinkQuest looks good on any school or college application," says Alperstein. "It shows that the students have been asking exceptional questions and working on independent projects since fifth grade."

"WHY SHOULD KIDS HAVE ALL THE FUN?"

In its second year of operation, ThinkQuest Junior started getting rave reviews from teachers. "I learned more from my ThinkQuest students than I learned in my master's program in distance education," one educator wrote. Another said, "In twelve years of teaching, few experiences rank higher than the ThinkQuest program. It was exhilarating and professionally challenging."

Encouraged by this feedback, we launched ThinkQuest for Tomorrow's Teachers, asking ourselves the question, Why should kids have all the fun? We offered more than $500,000 in cash awards to educators from grades K through 12 and announced that our goals were to

- Develop a new generation of teachers who would be technology literate;
- Empower educators to come up with their own vision to use computers and the Internet in class; and
- Foster collaboration between experienced teachers and future teachers.

We began by targeting the nation's leading schools of education, assuming that the next generation of teachers would be a lot more familiar with computers and much more at ease with technology. We were wrong. Education departments had very small budgets for technology, even for the smallest PCs. As a result, our newly trained teachers knew little about the Internet and even less about how to incorporate computers into the school curriculum.

We learned this, to our chagrin, at our awards ceremony. Linda Roberts chaired a panel that reviewed ThinkQuest International entries as well as those from ThinkQuest for Tomorrow's Teachers. While ThinkQuest kids were creating websites in multiple dimensions, most teachers couldn't think beyond PowerPoint, she noted. ThinkQuest kids were also used to multitasking and breezed through their presentations with ease, showing off their flash screens and interactive games, yet teachers found it difficult to talk about their subject matter and, at the same time, switch from one web page to another. The disparity between these groups was distressing. If we had judged all entries on the same scale, she noted, the ThinkQuest kids would have walked away with all the awards. Our ThinkQuest Junior entries were even more dynamic and imaginative!

Margaret Riel, a senior researcher in Technology and Education at SRI International and author of the white paper *The Future of Teaching*, had an explanation for this performance gap. "Teachers just don't have the leisure that kids do to explore this stuff," she said. "They're working nights and weekends grading papers, and have families as well. It's just a matter of free time."

We ran ThinkQuest for Tomorrow's Teachers for only one year. It was a disappointment—proving that adults have a hard time competing with the unfettered minds of kids. However, it affirmed my early intuition about computer education: If you want young people to learn a new technology, the best thing to do is to build them a big playground and let them make up their own games.

CHAPTER 12

MORPHING

Of course there is no formula for success except, perhaps, an unconditional acceptance of life and what it brings.

Arthur Rubinstein

OUR FALL 2000 THINKQUEST AWARDS CEREMONY was slated to be held in Cairo, and our host was to be Susan Mubarak, wife of the Egyptian president. Students and educators would be feted at the Opera House and the National Museum and then taken by camel to view the pyramids. Hisham El Sherif, one of Egypt's top venture capitalists, helped organize the festivities, and we invited ministers of education from more than twenty countries. However, in the months leading up to the event, the Middle East became a tinderbox.

In October, suicide bombers associated with Al-Qaeda blew up the USS *Cole*, stationed in the Yemeni port of Aden. A Palestinian mob murdered three Israeli soldiers, and in retribution the Israeli army attacked Palestinian targets in the West Bank and the Gaza Strip. In November, the Egyptian government rounded up members of the Muslim Brotherhood, setting off riots in the streets of Cairo. Just weeks before our scheduled departure later that month, the U.S. State Department told us Egypt wasn't safe.

At the time, we were working with educators to introduce Think-Quest in both Israel and Palestine, and we were about to sponsor an award for students who collaborated across conflicting borders. As the conflict heated up, many of the schools in Gaza were destroyed. The communications lines were down, and the project came to a halt.

Our most pressing problem was finding a replacement venue for the ThinkQuest awards and advising students of the change just weeks before they were scheduled to arrive in Cairo.

In Geneva, CERN was known for its spirit of collaboration. Throughout the Cold War, scientists from all countries gathered at CERN to work on common problems, and in the early 1990s, CERN had also given birth to the World Wide Web while Tim Berners-Lee was there. After a few phone calls to some colleagues at CERN, we got the green light to hold our awards ceremony there.

In March 2001—just a few months later than originally planned— our ThinkQuest finalists arrived in Geneva to accept awards for web-sites that addressed global problems from the looming energy crisis to health care to environmental threats. That year, Best of Contest went to a website on visual perception. Students asked: Can we trust our eyes? Is seeing believing? How many different versions are there of reality?

Secretary of State Madeleine Albright presented the Digital Diplomacy Award to students from the United States, England, and Hong Kong for their entry *An End to World Hunger: Hope for the Future*. Other award-winning websites focused on the world's great-est inventions, our progress in understanding the human genome, and leukemia.

That year we also partnered with the U.S. Department of Edu-cation's Community Technology Centers, HUD's Neighborhood Network, and Ability Awareness to reach across the digital divide, involving some 9.9 million students in poor schools, as well as kids with learning disabilities, in the ThinkQuest competition.

GROWING PAINS

The ThinkQuest library now contained four-thousand-plus student-created websites serving millions of teens around the globe. The contest had spread to 107 countries, and we were now giving away in excess of $1.5 million in scholarships every year. Yet our biggest success was about to become our biggest failure if we didn't make some serious fiscal changes. ANS was spending more than $6 million annually to operate this program. It was time to find a way to keep it going in the years to come.

Our first option was to go commercial. Major software companies were knocking at our door because we had the biggest educational portal on the Internet. A venture capital firm offered us $20 million for a majority share, but they planned to put ads on the site, and we didn't want to see a ThinkQuest page with pop-ups. We had worked hard to create a resource that students and educators could turn to, knowing with confidence that we would never try to sell them anything.

Linda Roberts then turned matchmaker, introducing us to the Oracle Education Foundation. We couldn't have been more fortunate in our new corporate sponsor. Oracle was already well known for its global educational efforts. Their computing platform, called Think. com, gave students in developing countries access to a potent mix of publishing, research, and social networking tools, and Oracle planned to funnel all these students into the ThinkQuest contest. After many discussions, we "donated" all of our ThinkQuest programs, except ThinkQuest NYC, which is covered in a later section, to the Oracle Foundation. In 2003, they took over the contest and made it part of their global education initiative.

REACHING ACROSS THE DIGITAL DIVIDE

Harry Tetteh was one of Oracle's early success stories, and one of Ghana's first ThinkQuest participants. Though Harry's high school had ten computers, the principal kept them locked up because he feared the students would damage them. Harry and his fellow classmates protested, and the principal relented, but the students were granted access for only a short period of time each day. To finish his ThinkQuest website, Harry worked at an Internet café twelve miles from his village, often until midnight. Once, as he walked home through the bush, he encountered a king cobra, its head raised and ready to strike. Often he went without food in order to buy computer time. Despite these hardships, Harry received a ThinkQuest award and went on to become one of his country's first computer consultants.

"If I had been told by a fortune-teller nine years ago that technology would be my career path," Harry told us, "I would have said certainly not. I had never even seen a computer. My goal was to stay in my village and help my grandfather run his cocoa farm. Now I am earning an online master's degree in Instructional and Educational Technology at National University in California."

Sigit Adinugroho was the first to enter the Oracle ThinkQuest program in Malaysia, working with students to explore the growing, processing, and marketing of coffee worldwide. "We consulted farmers in India, and they assisted us by providing photographs, news clippings, and information on coffee production. They treated us like family." In recent years, fair trade and humane working conditions have become important topics for ThinkQuest teams.

Jamaican student Jaevion Nelson created an award-winning website focusing on the United Nations' Millennium Development Goals dealing with hunger, child mortality, world health, and environmental sustainability. After receiving the Jamaican prime minister's Award for Excellence for international achievement, he began promoting computer education in his country's schools.

ThinkQuest students continue to draw our attention to the plight of children around the world. A compelling website profiles children who have been pressed into combat in Afghanistan, Colombia, Sierra Leone, and the Congo. *Young Blood: Children of War* reveals that there are now more than three hundred thousand soldiers under the age of fifteen involved in conflicts around the world.

Since 2005, the contest has grown dramatically in Romania, South Africa, Greece, Indonesia, and Spain, according to Orla Ni Chorcora, senior director of marketing of Oracle Education Initiatives. Fully two-thirds of its participants now come from countries outside the United States.

Recent entries explore the experience of immigration, Internet safety, censorship, and government ideologies. The winner of the 2008 competition, *Color Our World with Kindness*, was created by twelve-year-olds from Alabama and a small fishing village in Brazil. It opens with a rap song asking people to fight the impulse to despair and hate and to replace it with tolerance, forgiveness, and goodwill. Says Ni Chorcora, "This project is emblematic of twenty-first-century learning," combining an awareness of world problems with a compassionate response.

The ThinkQuest library continues to grow, and Oracle has made its more than seven thousand educational websites available to students around the world. It has also added new technology components that allow students to write their own blogs and use more advanced web applications.

ThinkQuest finalists are also making waves in the high-tech community, says Oracle's vice president of corporate citizenship, Claire Dolan. On a recent website, *Manufactured Minds,* a wisecracking robot provides a tour through the world of artificial intelligence (AI). The site covers AI basics and ethics, and it also includes a poetry quiz. Users have to guess whether a human or a computer has written the lines. "Once kids begin to work together," says Dolan, "they learn that they are capable of the kind of innovation that has given us cell phones and laptops." These students will be the leaders of our next high-tech revolution.

Equally important, ThinkQuest has shown how nonprofit organizations can change the educational system from without. What's more, this approach can work in every corner of the globe.

KEEPING PART OF THE MAGIC

Although we handed ThinkQuest International and ThinkQuest Junior over to Oracle, we held on to one small portion of the contest. We had just launched ThinkQuest NYC and believed we could make this spin-off financially independent. We also wanted to show how technology could transform urban schools. After 9/11, New York City's dropout rates were growing, and educators desperately needed ways to keep more than 1.1 million students engaged.

"It was a tough time to sell the contest," said ThinkQuest NYC Director Lisa Ernst. "Everyone was still grieving, and business had come to a halt. Yet in early 2002, Mayor Bloomberg announced his plans to revamp the education system." The Board of Education customized ThinkQuest NYC to meet their needs and approved a budget to train teachers how to administer it in over a hundred schools throughout the city.

One of our earliest entries came from the Gateway School, which educates children and teenagers with learning disabilities. An alumnus, Bill Reed, had developed an environmental education program to teach kids problem-solving and leadership skills. His students began studying the giant river otter, an endangered species native to South America. "Our fifth graders started corresponding with their counterparts in Guyana," says Reed, "and learned that the otter was competing with the residents for the local fish supply. One of our kids came up with a solution. He said, 'Why not build a fish pond, feed the villagers, and then give a portion of the fish to otters?' The government had come to the same conclusion. They set up the system, and it worked."

In the spring months of 2003, the Gateway team started to build a ThinkQuest website and began raising money to protect the otter. David Gustafson, who lost his mother on 9/11, threw himself into the project, designing T-shirts with an image of this endangered creature on them. Sales of the shirts netted $2,500 to help preserve the animals. His teammate, Madelaine Greenbaum, a shy girl who could barely talk in class, addressed members of the Philadelphia Zoo, describing the otter population and its river habitat.

In June 2004, the Gateway students won first place. No one—not even the judges—knew these kids were coping with attention deficit disorder and dyslexia.

A NEW INCARNATION

ANS has donated more than $1.7 million in matching grants to ThinkQuest NYC. The program has engaged more than twenty-five thousand students and trained thousands of teachers from both public and private schools. It has had a significant impact on the educational system, as well as on the individual participants, and it has been referred to as an economic wonder.

In 2009, the organization broadened its portfolio, cosponsoring a digital media academy with NBC and an online journalism award with *The Jim Lehrer NewsHour* on PBS. The organization also encourages students to create films and public service announcements, as well as websites devoted to charity. Under the direction of its new executive director, Barbara Colwell, it will explore corporate internships and entrepreneurship classes for students in grades 5 through 12.

Leaders in the high-tech industry will keep ThinkQuest NYC abreast of new technologies. Says Michael Wehner, managing director of Media and Entertainment Solutions at Microsoft, "Websites aren't enough. We're starting to look at mashups, applications that allow users to integrate information from a variety of sources, including maps from Google, news feeds from other websites, music from iTunes, and video captured by a cell phone. Students can post this information on their homepage or on YouTube."

Adds Wehner, "Technology is no longer for the geeky students. Our platforms are now accessible to all. That means our emphasis needs to be on the richness of information and new ways of sharing it."

Futurist Edie Weiner, who chairs the ThinkQuest NYC board, has a long track record of predicting social trends; she wants to be sure that students stay ahead of the curve. "Right now, we're looking at how virtual reality will affect the American economy, how we conduct business meetings and courtship, and how our new technology will impact everything from brain research to education and religion," she says. "We need to prepare young people to deal with these trends in the workplace and in their daily lives."

PART THREE

What Is Reality?

CHAPTER 13

DESIGNING THE VIRTUAL CLASSROOM

Reality is merely an illusion, albeit a very persistent one.

Albert Einstein

WHILE WE WERE RUNNING THINKQUEST, we were also creating the next generation of computer technology. ANS provided the engineers and architects for Internet2, developing a network with even greater speed and capacity to serve the nation's universities and research labs. At the same time, we developed a very sophisticated program to measure the quality of service on the Internet. We issued report cards on ISPs, grading their overall performance. And most important, we began to build the classroom of the future—a way to bring three-dimensional computer education right into the home.

There's a saying, "Science fiction doesn't remain so for long—at least not on the Internet." By the 1990s, computer worlds were no longer confined to a flat twelve-inch monitor. They could incorporate the elements of sound, smell, and touch, allowing us to create a learning environment akin to the *Star Trek* holodeck.

THE ADVENT OF TELE-IMMERSION

From 1996 to 2001, ANS led and funded the National Tele-Immersion Initiative to connect users at a distance and allow them to play in the same virtual world. Our dream was to create the illusion that people in different places were present in the same room and then let them use any computer backgrounds and simulations they desired to create the reality they chose.

As builders of the Internet, we saw the potential for this new technology to change the way we learn. Tele-immersion is a technology that does exactly what its name implies: It engages all the senses and totally immerses us in our subject matter. And it can be used to create a variety of scenarios and learning environments. The beauty of tele-immersion is that it involves the whole body and mind in the learning process. Chemistry no longer has to be about memorizing tables and abstract properties. Instead, students can walk into a tele-cubicle and interact with an atomic structure that's projected in three dimensions. Using a robotic glove, they can actually feel the forces that hold the molecules together.

Educators believe that tele-immersion will eventually do away with textbooks and allow kids to step inside a problem and see it from the inside out, making learning more visceral and intuitive. It will also engage a greater portion of the brain—not just the area responsible for logic and linear thought but also the areas that deal with spatial relationships and visual and kinesthetic memory.

Back in 1996, however, our goal was to create the first national demonstration of this new technology and show how it might enhance creativity and collaboration. As the chief architects and engineering group for Internet2, ANS had access to very high bandwidth, and we were able to use that bandwidth for our experiments. Tele-immersion is the most challenging application of all because it pushes both the speed and the latency (the delay between transmission and reception) of a network to the outer limits.

The Players and the Process

This project would require the collaboration of computer scientists, mathematicians, network pioneers, and most important, experts in virtual reality. Until ANS funded this national initiative, however, many of these groups worked in isolation. Most competed for funds rather than collaborating on big multidisciplinary problems. To counteract this siloization, we promised our colleagues that any specifications or applications we developed for this project would be open source—that is, they would be available to all universities and researchers at no charge.

In October 1996, we sponsored the first conference on tele-immersion at the University of Illinois–Urbana-Champaign, inviting a small group of researchers from universities, industry, and the top national labs across the country. The University of Illinois had already replicated objects in a room in three dimensions using Cave Automated Virtual Environment (CAVE) technology. This acronym was a tongue-in-cheek reference to Plato's parable of the cave in *The Republic*, a discourse on the nature of illusion and reality.

Experts from other universities were experimenting with avatars, robotics, and information sharing on multiple computers. Their applications included programs for tele-medicine, national defense, the NASA space program, and grade-school classrooms. When I asked the many present who the best person would be to lead this initiative, the answer was Jaron Lanier, a thirty-six-year-old autodidact who invented the term *virtual reality* and patented the robotic glove for video gamers. A genius and a true visionary, Lanier was respected by all.

Working closely with Fred Brooks at the University of North Carolina, as well as with teams at Caltech, Carnegie Mellon, and other sites, Lanier constructed a telecubicle, a desk with two converging screens that created a three-dimensional model of reality. Our goal was to combine the visuals at two or more sites to create the sense that both parties were working together in the same room. But creating the illusion of co-presence wasn't easy. To explain why, we need to consider the history of videoconferencing and the reasons it has never quite caught on.

SOLVING THE SUBTLETIES

Split-screen visuals have been with us for quite a while. In the 1950s, Bell Labs set up the first visual link from New York to Washington, just before the advent of television, and by the 1990s, several companies were promoting videoconferencing. Most people used this tool for about six months and then abandoned it. Why? The program omitted critical visual details. As Lanier explains, "An ordinary video link upsets part of the brain that is looking for subtle cues." If the transmission isn't fast enough—with even a fraction of a millisecond delay—the eyes grow tired. So does the brain, because it's constantly trying to fill in the blanks and create a more faithful representation of reality.

Such facial expressions as the raising of an eyebrow or a slight grimace are crucially important, and we depend on them to analyze a person's emotional state. But most videoconferencing programs don't pick them up, thereby leaving us feeling vaguely uneasy about our interactions. For a program to be successful in the long term, it must have a high resolution and allow us to read the minutest of gestures.

Tele-immersion was the first program to capture these subtle cues, and it set a standard that has yet to be met by other immersive environments today.[13]

We managed it through a series of individual experiments that integrated all the senses. Our first job was to translate onto a mathematical grid what viewers were seeing. To capture a person sitting at a conference table, for example, we employed multiple cameras and combined views from different angles. This allowed us to create a sculptural model of reality. Our first mathematical models were unreliable; they were easily thrown off by a blank wall that seemed to the cameras to have no apparent shape or depth. Early digital photography simply couldn't "read" a white space on a wall any better than it could read a stark white T-shirt or a bright spot on a human face. The human brain doesn't interpret white as infinity cameras do.

Researchers at the University of North Carolina–Chapel Hill solved this problem by filling the computer area with imperceptible structured light (ISL). "This appears to the naked eye as a continuous source of illumination, yet it's actually filling the room with quickly changing patterns," says Lanier. "This allows us to fill in the void produced by white walls with other features." The use of ISL thus allowed our sea of cameras to incorporate the blank wall into their measurements. In technical terms, we were the first to accurately measure the depth of a pixel and create a volumetric version of reality.

Images from the individual telecubicles were then transmitted to a computer processor that combined the visuals. We layered images of participants at different sites, so it appeared that everyone was present in the same room.

Our first users also wore special headsets to achieve "stereo vision," just like views of the first three-dimensional movies, and the results were remarkably realistic.

Our next challenge was in the realm of touch: orchestrating the first tele-immersion handshake across a distance of some 540 miles. To achieve this, we didn't have to rely on a robotic glove. All we had to do was supply the visuals. Participants had the sensation of shaking hands because their brains assumed they were doing so, based on visual cues. "This is how things work in a virtual world," says Lanier. "If we project an image of your hands on a table, you will have the accompanying sensation. It's somewhat akin to an amputee who reports feeling in a phantom limb."

Lanier described all our attempts to reproduce human interaction as a kind of stage magic. "Doing a perfect job is out of the question," he said. "So we do an imperfect job, knowing the brain is able to fill in the blanks.

"It's a little bit like sleight of hand," he added. "If you want something to seem to work perfectly, you distract the brain for a second. You put on a good show, and go for a major cognitive effect."

Next we tried to reproduce the sense of smell. Lanier had investigated olfactory perception with neuroscientist Jim Bower at Caltech,[14] and Bower had noted that smell enables us to make a wide range of judgments about our environment and our relationships. Of all the senses, it's the oldest and most complex. "The others involve only a few fundamental processes," explained Lanier. "Color, for example, has three kinds of receptors in the brain. Sound breaks down into a certain manageable set of frequencies. But olfaction is a catalogue of thousands upon thousands of scents. These are linked not only to memory but to the development of language, and to the biology of desire and attraction."

At that time, computer simulations of smell were unreliable. We tested one program that released an odor into the tele-immersion environment only to find that it wasn't that easy to disperse! Users would also have to wear nose clips, and we felt that that would be a distraction. We settled for reproducing sight, sound, and touch, relying on the brain's capacity to read things on the periphery of experience, and left olfaction for other researchers to sort out.

Improvements at Every Level

In May 2000, we demonstrated our first link among three locations: the University of North Carolina in Chapel Hill, the University of Pennsylvania in Philadelphia, and ANS headquarters in Armonk, New York. The only problem was some "noise" in the system that looked like confetti falling inside the cubicles.

Six months later, we had removed the confetti and improved the quality and speed of the system, allowing researchers from Brown

University to bring virtual objects into the simulation. This time government and industry officials were in attendance. Lanier sat at a cubicle at ANS headquarters and Robert Zeleznick sat in a similar cubicle in Providence, Rhode Island, yet on the computer screen, both men appeared to be occupying the same office. Using virtual tools, they proceeded to create their own furniture—adding a meeting table and some chairs—and then altered the dimensions of the room. This demonstration showed that we now had the power to create worlds that were half virtual and half real.

Although this was a major breakthrough, it would take a while for this technology to reach a wider audience. For one thing, the process was a voracious consumer of computer resources. Dozens of refrigerator-sized processors were required to project a three-dimensional model of reality. Even more were needed to render the scene from shifting perspectives and to follow each user's head as it moved throughout the session. Lanier often joked about the "number of refrigerators" we had to hook up to achieve a certain level of fidelity. An eight-processor cluster cost between $30,000 and $50,000, bringing the total to about $150,000 for every telecubicle. This made tele-immersion about a hundred times too expensive to compete with other communication technologies.

There were design problems to be solved as well. Engineers would have to deal with latency, reducing the time elapsed between transmission and reception, because the virtual world operates effectively only if information is received within 30 to 50 milliseconds after it is generated. Any longer, and the result is disorientation. The user may even experience nausea as the illusion degrades. Even Internet2 had some difficulty transmitting such complex data without any snags or interruptions.

Ideally, the next incarnation of tele-immersion would also do away with cumbersome three-dimensional headsets. Instead, it would use autostereo, a program used by the aviation industry in cockpit displays.

That said, there were many reasons to fast-track this technology. Chief among them was the coming fuel crisis. Travel was becoming more expensive; in addition, it was also more damaging to the environment. World health experts also linked it with the rapid transmission of diseases like avian flu. Yet tele-immersion could reduce the need for on-site meetings and enhance online collaboration in a wide range of professions.

ANOTHER WAVE OF THE FUTURE

As the developers of this technology, we envisioned a brave new world where surgeons would guide their colleagues, and even their robots, through complex operations from a distance. Architects would make major changes in building design without having to go on-site or coordinate five sets of blueprints. Archaeologists would be able to "sit in" on remote digs from the comfort of their living rooms. NASA engineers would be able to address operating problems on a space shuttle from the safety of mission headquarters. This technology would also revolutionize distance education. Our best teachers would reach a larger audience, making eye contact with their viewers. One day, telecubicles would be built large enough to accommodate music and theater audiences, because this new technology is capable of conveying all the nuances of a live performance.

In 2001, the *Los Angeles Times* predicted that tele-immersion would lead to a new wave of innovation. "The telecubicle offers a glimpse of the Internet of the future—one that will be liberated from computer monitors and infused with the essential senses of sight, sound, and touch . . . computer-generated avatars will become realistic stand-ins for actual people . . . and force-feedback technology will reveal the shape and texture of physical objects across a computer network."[15]

ANS spent roughly $10 million to get these new technologies off the ground. And over the past eight years, NSF has invested more than $16 million in tele-immersion, working with the University of Southern California (USC) to make this dream into a reality. At present, USC investigators are studying the details of facial expression—the sly smile, the sarcastic roll of the eyes—so computer models can provide us with better clues about a person's emotional state. These researchers are also making advances in haptics, or the "technology of touch," that, for example, will allow users of a museum website to feel the surface of a Grecian urn and let online shoppers feel the texture of a coat or shirt. A program called Cybergrasp will also aid in the rehabilitation of stroke patients and provide "visualization exercises" for the blind.[16]

Tim O'Reilly, a blogger who watches the alpha geeks to determine emerging technology trends, has said, "The network is opening up some amazing possibilities for us to reinvent content, reinvent collaboration." This will promote innovation across the board and give us more "eureka" moments.

PART FOUR

Social Entrepreneurs

CHAPTER 14

A NEW KIND OF PHILANTHROPY

I've always said that the better off you are, the more responsibility you have for helping others. Just as I think it's important to run companies well, with a close eye to the bottom line, I think you have to use your entrepreneurial experience to make corporate philanthropy effective.

Carlose Slim Helu

BY 2004, ANS HAD DONE great things as a nonprofit. We had helped build the Internet and introduced young people around the world to the magic of online collaboration. And we had funded the classroom of the future, using next wave technology. Our mission going forward was to enter the realm of philanthropy, supporting organizations that could close the opportunity gap and make American youth both computer and information literate.

The company had spent easily and freely in boom times and had to decide at that juncture how to make the best use of its remaining assets. First, we decided to close our headquarters in Armonk and set up a virtual office, using cell phones and computers. This way we could reduce our overhead and put every penny into helping kids.

Second, we started looking for organizations that already had a track record in this area. ANS had made most of its advances through strategic partnerships, and so we wanted to ally ourselves with others who were working toward the same goal as we were. As we moved into the realm of philanthropy, we wanted to invest in sustainable giving, supporting organizations that would be around for generations to come.

THE LEARNING CURVE

This was new territory for our board, and we came up with a plan to give them hands-on training. The concept was simple but effective. We asked every ANS board member to fund a community project related to education and technology and then to use their expertise and contacts to help that enterprise become self-sufficient and stand on its own. This was exactly the reverse of the way most nonprofits operate. The boards are usually expected to raise money and bring in donations from outside sources. Instead, ANS asked its board to give money away, starting with a $10,000 check to a charitable program. If their projects did well, our support would escalate. In the meantime, everyone would learn how hard it is to find and mentor worthy programs.

We expected all the board members to give a progress report one year out, in front of their peers. Because no one wanted to explain to the group why he or she had failed, everybody made extremely careful choices and devoted many hours to their adopted programs. Within two years, the ANS board and management were completely in sync and had developed a new approach to giving. We not only wrote out checks, we also identified the ways we could help each organization using our contacts and our technical and business expertise.

This approach worked so well that we now advise all nonprofits to involve their boards in the same way. Though our initial board grants were for $10,000, this figure can be adjusted. Large nonprofits can give more, smaller ones less, but the guidelines for targeted giving remain the same: Find an organization with similar goals, a solid business plan, and a good staff; then figure out how you can help them grow.

To our delight, all the board members chose to follow their own passion.

Board Members as Philanthropists

CFO Harris took the PC Users Group in Sarasota, Florida, under his wing, helping a group of volunteers collect and refurbish old computers and distribute them to low-income students and community organizations. In its early years, the PC Users Group provided hundreds of computers to low-income schoolchildren, to single mothers trying to further their own education, and to organizations serving local retirees. This group, with roughly a thousand members, now offers unlimited classes in everything from email management to photo workshops to understanding Windows Vista for only $35 a month. Harris, who also served as treasurer of the organization, helped this group set up this educational program, which offers courses for less than a third of what a community college might charge.

At the same time, I discovered Ron Zimmerman, a teacher and tech consultant who rebuilt computers in his garage in his spare time and then distributed them to grade-school students, and I started him off with an ANS board grant. As Zimmerman's project grew, so did our support. In 2006, we decided to create a more formal program with Sarasota's Education Foundation, the charitable arm of our local Department of Education. Each year, the TeXellence program provides computers to more than a thousand fourth graders and is one of the most successful projects of its kind in the country.

ANS has since provided Sarasota's Education Foundation with more than $450,000 in seed funds to better serve the Sarasota schools. Each time we renewed our grant, we did so with the proviso that they obtain matching funds from the community. Now supported by Dart

Foundation, the Community Foundation of Venice, and several local businesses, the Sarasota Education Foundation has enough pledges to support it for the next two years.

Board member Myra Williams was among the first in the pharmaceutical industry to use computer models in the design of drugs, first as director of R&D at Merck and, later, as vice president of Glaxo Wellcome. Despite her busy schedule, Williams always took time to tutor high school students. She used her first ANS board grant to set up computer labs for the Learning Connection, a nonprofit that allowed students with health problems to take courses online. Then Williams started looking for another organization to mentor.

In the university town of Princeton, New Jersey, she discovered a surprising need. About one-third of the public school students were black or Hispanic. They came from subsidized housing, and most of them needed a safe environment in which to study.

Williams helped a group called Princeton Young Achievers address this problem by creating an after-school computer literacy program along the lines of ThinkQuest—one that would teach teamwork and multidisciplinary learning and give these students strategies to succeed in the real world. She also volunteered her own expertise as a researcher to document the impact of the program and attract more funders.

Board member Jim McGroddy is a physicist and former senior vice president of science and technology at IBM Research. He attributes much of his success to the Jesuit prep school he attended in Regis, New York. In 2004, he learned that the Jesuit-run Cristo Rey School in Manhattan was targeting low-income kids and offering a unique work-study plan. The student body was divided into groups of five students, and each group shared a full-time job. This meant that each student put in one day every week at the job site. Combined, the groups' paychecks cover 70 percent of the school's operating costs, and the students get a foothold in the business world, interning at some of the nation's most prestigious corporations and nonprofits.

McGroddy immediately offered his services as a tech adviser and used an ANS board grant to get every student a home computer. The following year, his board grant provided all the school's students with thumb drives so they could easily ferry data back and forth between home and school. With his third ANS board grant, McGroddy set up a computer lab with the latest Mac equipment. (Over the years, McGroddy supplemented the board grants with his own money. In fact, he gave more over time from his own pocket than ANS provided in its three grants.)

The classroom experience is now very rich technologically. Cristo Rey students all know how to control a projector from their laptops, make a strong business presentation, and use the latest software in their jobs.

Inspired by ANS, McGroddy has started a family foundation to pass on the practice of giving to his adult children. "I've learned that a small amount of money and a personal commitment can go a long way," he says.

As executive vice chancellor and CFO of the California State University campuses, Richard West helped guide ANS in the field of computer education. He used his ANS grants to reach children of migrant workers and to help Hispanic students in Los Angeles—two communities he hoped to attract to the California state college system.

West's first board grant went to connect a grade school in the desert to the JASON Project, an online program that allows grade-school students to participate in major scientific expeditions as they are unfolding. This project relies on tele-immersion, the three-dimensional computer application ANS helped develop. Our grant allowed West to bus students from the town of Desert Sands, near Palm Springs, to an auditorium on the California State University–San Bernardino campus, where they were able to interact with scientists online and meet with Dr. Robert Ballard, the discoverer of the *Titanic* and founder and chairman of the JASON Project.

The Desert Sands school district encompassed families living in extreme poverty and in extreme affluence, West explained. Migrant workers often brought their children to school after the harvest in October and then took them out again in May. Teachers had only a short time in which to engage these students. The JASON Project provided many with their most dramatic learning experience. One Hispanic eighth grader was invited to explore the jungles of Panama with the project's research team the following summer.

West then looked for another way to use ANS seed money to help urban youth. This time, he worked with the educational arm of TELACU, the largest community development corporation in the United States. TELACU is headquartered in Los Angeles, where the dropout rate is among the highest in the country. Its goal is to keep Hispanic kids in school by providing them with computer training, scholarships, and mentoring.

In 2007, an ANS board grant helped upgrade TELACU's Tech Center in order to help students from low-income families better prepare for the SAT and wade through the college application process. The following year, West linked TELACU to a California State University program that was teaching Internet literacy.

"It takes more than scholarships to keep our kids in school," TELACU Industries president and CEO Michael Lizarraga told us. "What they need is encouragement and a worldview that embraces education as the pathway to success. Our TELACU Scholar program is now supporting between four hundred and five hundred students, with a 100 percent retention and graduation rate. Graduates are then placed at the local banks and health-care institutions that partner with the TELACU Foundation. And the biggest winner of all is the community."

"Start locally" was the motto of ANS secretary Kristin Mortensen, who found a worthy project to support in her own backyard. In 2005, Mortensen, who had been my assistant for almost twenty-five years,

A New Kind of Philanthrophy   121

asked for help creating a computer lab at the Sarah Hull Hallock Free Library in her hometown of Milton, New York, in the heart of the Hudson Valley. "When I tried to put up a poster for ThinkQuest," she reminded us, "the library didn't have any equipment, and no one could participate. Now they have a couple of monster desktops that are out of date, and it's easy to trip over the wires as you come up the stairs."

With an ANS board grant, the library purchased several workstations, some computer training, and a wireless hookup. When the local teenagers started using the computer lab as a gathering place after school, the library reserved two computers "for adults only" and placed them in a separate room.

"The atmosphere of the library has changed completely," Mortensen reports. "It's now a gathering place for students to do their homework. A lot of them don't have computers at home. They not only learn how to surf the Net, they get exposed to books as well."

The local library was an important place for Mortensen and her four siblings when they were growing up. "In the 1960s," she said, "the library was our information highway." When asked if she found it hard to mentor an organization, Mortensen replied, "Not really. I had been with ANS for so long, I'd seen other people do it. Our company has always been about helping others. For years, all I did was write out checks and watch worthy projects grow."

PRACTICE WORKS

In a very short time, the entire ANS board became experts at the practice of sustainable giving. They were able to review our funding recommendations with a greater understanding of the art of giving and to respond knowledgeably about and quickly to every major project we proposed. ANS has now supported better than thirty organizations and spent in excess of $5 million using technology as a lever to help disadvantaged youth.

The following chapters show donors of every stripe how they can give strategically, help an organization attract a larger base of funding, and affect the national dialogue on education and antipoverty initiatives.

I've chosen three case histories—Computers for Youth, the National Foundation for Teaching Entrepreneurship, and Year Up—to show how with less than $1 million each, ANS helped these organizations increase their audience or rise to national prominence.

CHAPTER 15

BRINGING TECHNOLOGY INTO THE HOME

It is every man's obligation to put back into the world at least the equivalent of what he takes out of it.

Albert Einstein

AS ANS MOVED INTO the realm of philanthropy, the American dream was in danger of collapsing. High school dropout rates were on the rise, and so was poverty. One-third of American students had failed to receive a high school diploma and were headed for dead-end jobs at the lowest end of the pay scale. They were also more likely to engage in illegal activities or be involved in a teenage pregnancy, according to the American Policy Institute.

Low-income students were six times more likely to drop out than their peers. African American students from poor neighborhoods had the lowest graduation rates: Only 50 percent completed high school, compared to 53 percent for Hispanics.

The most alarming finding was that for children of immigrants, things did not improve over time. Academic performance didn't increase in the second and third generation, even though these families now had higher incomes and parents had more stable jobs.[17] According to a report by the Educational Testing Service (one of the largest and most respected educational companies in the world), the earning power of high school dropouts had steadily decreased by 35 percent during the previous three decades.[18]

ANS had the money to make a difference, but we did not want to waste time and energy starting new programs from scratch. We wanted to leverage our investments to get the biggest return for every dollar. The best way to accomplish this was by helping other organizations that were already doing good work. We would use our management expertise and our contacts to help them reach a larger audience.

SELECTING THE RIGHT CANDIDATE

As the word got out, we were inundated with requests for help. Finally, we had to announce a change: "No more unsolicited proposals. We're changing the rules. We'll go out and identify organizations with good management. Then we'll figure out how to make them grow." Our initial research took months and generated stacks of material, but finally some good candidates rose to the top.

Among them was New York City's Computers for Youth (CFY). ThinkQuest had proven that computers empower kids and engage them in the learning process. The contest also had encouraged participants to mentor students from low-income schools. This organization appealed to us because it had a sustainable model for getting computers and the Internet into low-income homes. So we decided to interview the people who had started it.

In 1998, New York attorney Dan Dolgin learned that 15 million computers were thrown away each year; concurrently, 15 million

American children were living below the poverty line. He proposed to solve both problems by updating those machines and giving them to inner-city kids. That year, he partnered with Elisabeth Stock, a technology expert who believed in educating entire families, to launch Computers for Youth.

Stock was an inspired choice to get this program off the ground. After graduating from MIT with degrees in writing and engineering, she joined the Peace Corps in West Africa and learned what a powerful role education plays in alleviating poverty. Stock later worked for the World Bank, introducing technology to Africa. After receiving two master's degrees (one in urban studies, another in technology and public policy), she became a White House fellow where, in 1996, she was the principal architect of a program that enables federal agencies to donate surplus computers directly to needy schools. The problem, as she explained to us, was that this program had no teeth. The schools just didn't have the resources to teach technology. The Justice Department sent a carload of computers to a local school, but they sat in the basement because the principal had no idea what to do with them. Stock was certain these computers would get more use in an informal setting.

"When I was at MIT in 1986, the college gave us email accounts, believing that the best place to infuse technology was in a casual context," she said. "There were computer stands all around the campus, and we had access from the libraries, the cafeterias, and [the] dorms. Our universities had wisely created a learning environment that extended beyond the classroom and embraced all aspects of campus life. Why not use this same approach to introduce grade-school students to the wonders of technology?

"If we could give educational games and software they could use at home," she added, "learning would become fun and start involving the whole family. Students would become mentors both for their parents and their younger siblings, and this would build their self-esteem."

In 1998, Stock left the White House to create the first and most comprehensive effort to date to bring technology into the home. As CFY's president and COO, she provided families of grade-school students with computers, training, tech support, and educational software, along with discounted access to the Internet.

"Educators said we were headed in the wrong direction," Stock recalled. "They had trouble getting parents to show up at PTA meetings and said we'd be lucky to get ten parents to attend a workshop. But we saw that the after-school environment was a huge untapped opportunity."

Compared to the classroom or the after-school center, the home has received little attention from policy makers and educators, yet this is where children spend the greatest amount of time. Studies show that the average grade-school student spends only 13 out of every 100 hours in the classroom. We knew from our years of running ThinkQuest that students have the leisure to experiment with technology at home and that they learn more about how the equipment works than they would at a school computer lab or library. Moreover, researchers had also begun to see that parental involvement in the learning experience is critical.

Each year, private foundations and the government spend millions to help low-income families through programs like Head Start and educational media like *Sesame Street*, which prepare low-income and minority children for kindergarten. Yet, our nation provides virtually no support for at-home learning by the time children reach middle school. Significantly, this is when educators see the steepest decline in academic performance. Research has revealed a disturbing correlation between reduced attention at home and a drop in test scores for students entering sixth grade.

COMPUTERS TO GO

In 1999, CFY began handing out computers to grade-schoolers and their families in Harlem, Brooklyn, and the Bronx. Major corporations like Time Warner and Goldman Sachs donated the machines. Volunteers and vocational tech students helped refurbish them, doing the necessary repairs and updates. CFY then held Saturday workshops to teach families to set up and maintain their desktops. While only a handful of parents showed up for the traditional parent-teacher night, these Saturday tech workshops drew more than a hundred families.

CFY also hosted Family Tech Nights throughout the year, teaching parents how to use the latest educational software. Master teachers showed families how to do research on the Web, to play games that hone reading and problem-solving skills, and to use the Internet to help with health care and financial planning. Sixth-grade teachers received the same machines and software, allowing them to track assignments and monitor their students' progress. As their grades and test scores improved, students also gained a better understanding of the kind of jobs available in an information economy. All of a sudden children who didn't feel as if they had a role in society were saying, "Maybe there *is* a place for me."

ANS MONEY ALLOWS FOR EXPANSION

CFY was just the kind of innovative program we wanted to support. It had strong leadership, a solid business plan, and an impressive track record.

When CFY opened its doors, 40 percent of low-income families had no Internet access, and African American and Hispanic families tended to use the Internet less than whites and Asians. Within a year, Stock had lined up an array of blue-chip partners including Microsoft, Citigroup, and Ivillage.com to help change that demographic.

THE MAKING OF A MASTER TEACHER

Berkis Cruz Eusebio, an energetic woman with large almond-shaped eyes and an engaging smile, became a master teacher after participating in CFY with her son, Daniel.

"Daniel was bright, but he had a hard time reading," she recalls. "I saw the difference a computer could make for kids like him who were struggling academically. And I discovered that CFY games and software taught important decision-making skills."

In a game called "Rescue Mission," Daniel and his classmates used military strategies to deliver food and first aid to trouble spots around the world. "This program taught kids the value of helping other countries and of strategies other than going to war," Eusebio says.

Soon Daniel began working as a volunteer, reading to patients at a local hospital. Today, he maintains an A-minus average and participates in poetry slams, even though he used to dread writing assignments. "Communication now comes easily to him," reports his mother. "For Daniel and for so many others, the computer was the missing link to good performance."

Inspired by her son's transformation, Eusebio became a master teacher, offering training sessions in English and in her native Spanish. She brings a wide range of experience to the job. For eleven years, Eusebio served as a recruiting coordinator at Columbia University, helping graduating seniors interview for prospective jobs. She then joined Help USA, working to bring the homeless back into the economic mainstream. "It was a big switch, going from Ivy League students to people born to a life of poverty," she says. "Suddenly I was counseling families who were trying to raise their kids on no resources. This helped me understand the mission of CFY—and the importance of giving a boost to those who really need it."

In the 1990s, African American and Hispanic families in poor neighborhoods were less likely to know how to surf the Net or research a homework problem than families in the middle class were. Volunteers like Eusebio are changing that. They put parents at ease while they show them how to help their children learn.

"Many are immigrants and don't know English very well," says CFY president and COO Elisabeth Stock. "Some may never have stepped inside a classroom. But all of them want the same thing: a better future for their kids."

A fearless and effective fund-raiser, Stock spoke to corporate backers about the need to raise the bar for urban youth. She also understood economies of scale. The first year, CFY spent $850 per family, providing them with upgraded computers, training, and software. The cost per family dropped to less than $400 as CFY reached a wider audience. This was a combination of the volume going up—thus giving CFY some leverage with its fixed costs—and the staff learning how to focus on their variable costs—which they improved at quickly. A continuing decline in computer prices makes the program even more cost-effective as time goes on. As Chip Raymond, president of the Citigroup Foundation, told the *Wall Street Journal,* "Elisabeth has a business plan you could [have started] a billion-dollar company with."

In September 2004, we decided to help take this program national. We offered to provide $1.3 million in seed money, which would allow CFY to set up branches in four other cities. Our primary requirements were that the CFY obtain matching grants in each new city and that each office become self-sustaining within the first two years.

Stock immediately set to work. She evaluated more than ten cities as possible candidates. Her criteria were *market size*—the city had to have a large enough low-income population to allow CFY to benefit from economies of scale; *community support*—the desire of the school superintendent and other key power brokers to back the program; *applicability*—the city must be somewhat typical so that CFY could apply lessons learned in New York and other markets; and *qualified personnel*—a local talent pool from which to hire a tech staff and a strong administrator.

Chicago was CFY's initial target, and the local school board was eager to match our grants. At the last minute, however, administrators discovered a shortfall in their budget; the launch would have to be delayed. Stock moved on to CFY's second choice, Boston, only to discover that the city had just committed to another tech-education project. The first candidate with both funding and strong local support was Philadelphia. CFY opened a branch there that is now serving more than a thousand families and doubling its audience each year. The schools were spread out over a larger area than Stock had anticipated, so it took more effort to reach low-income families. CFY acted responsibly, cutting back on its infrastructure to keep expenses down until the program could get rolling.

In Atlanta, Stock invited local educators and members of the tech industry to serve on an honorary board and thus help the program build a strong base of support.

But the biggest success came in California in fall 2008. CFY received an Emerging Technology grant from the state in the amount of $750,000, allowing it to establish two new offices—one in the San Francisco Bay Area and the other in Los Angeles.

ANS had allocated $250,000 in seed funds for each new location, and CFY was able to attract matching donors in every new community it served.

A MORE RESILIENT STYLE OF LEARNING

One of the key elements in CFY's expansion was its growing reputation for research. Stock now had her own data showing that home computer education improved test scores, increased self-reliance and self-confidence, and provided for greater family support of each student's academic and life goals.

"The computer has proven to be a wonderful tool for self-remediation," reports Kallen Tsikalis, CFY's director of research. "Kids think, 'I'll keep trying until I get my score up.' The bottom line is that the computer builds a tolerance for failure and a more resilient attitude."

This stick-to-itiveness is crucial for kids who are struggling to catch up with their peers. The computer is noncritical and private: It allows students to test themselves without fear of humiliation. And educational software encourages students to keep on working until they get results.

Carol Dweck, professor of psychology at Stanford University, has told educators that it's more important to build a more resilient style of learning than it is to peg children according to their IQs and test scores. Tsikalis recently conducted a study of effort versus innate intelligence using CFY students. The results: After using math software for seventeen hours, sixth graders improved their test scores and their self-confidence. "With computers we have a silver bullet," Tsikalis says. "We're learning how to eradicate the belief, 'I can't do this,' and replace it with a positive attitude."

CHARTING STUDENT ENGAGEMENT

Motivation is now a big buzzword in the educational community and a major focus of the Educational Testing Service. ANS introduced this organization to CFY, noting that it had a good handle on what makes low-income students more likely to succeed in college. The Educational Testing Service is now collaborating with CFY on an ambitious three-year study to show how students become engaged—and stay engaged—in the learning process.

At the same time, policy makers are also beginning to realize that they can get the best bang for their buck by investing in the home learning environment. CFY's latest study shows that children learn more when they play online games with their parents.

Yet there appears to be a ripple effect that goes beyond the family. One in every three CFY students also reported that they have stronger relationships with their peers and find it easier to make friends. Others cited increased relaxation, greater curiosity, and a sense of having more control over their lives as important benefits of their computer learning at home.

CFY AMBASSADORS

As CFY enters phase two of its expansion, targeting Chicago and Boston, Stock is drawing on recent CFY graduates to help sell the program. Among her current ambassadors are seventh grader Diamone Moon, who turned to the Internet to research the tap dancing style of Gregory Hines. Since participating in CFY, Diamone has become a proficient typist, and now she routinely uses the computer to help her check dates and facts for school reports.

Seventh grader Mercedes Aguilar [a pseudonym] is using her computer to tell the story of her journey across the Texas border with an older cousin. At age five, Mercedes saw dead bodies in the desert, and she had to go from house to house asking for food. She's writing about this passage, she says, "so others will understand what it's like to be an immigrant." The computer has helped her family improve their English and prepare for their citizenship tests.

A NATIONAL VOICE

In 2005, ANS suggested that CFY develop a road map for other organizations serving low-income youth. Stock came up with a plan to build a network of affiliates, sharing CFY's expertise in home computer learning and its top educational software. Over the past ten years, CFY has worked with companies like RiverDeep, Read Please, Sun Microsystems, and Scholastic to develop more effective teaching tools for low-income families. "Our goal is to make our basic software package available to our affiliates in fifty states," says Stock, "and to raise public awareness of the home learning environment."

ANS was pleased to bring in CFY's first affiliate member: the Education Foundation of Sarasota, Florida. We even sent representatives from its Department of Education to CFY headquarters for training. Through the affiliate program, CFY plans to create a grassroots network that can influence educational policy on both national and local levels.

A BLUEPRINT FOR THE FUTURE

Fifteen years ago, no one understood how to bring disadvantaged kids into the mainstream. Schools were overcrowded and teachers overtaxed. Administrators and software developers didn't have much leeway—everything they did was geared to "teaching to the test."

ThinkQuest got around this problem by going directly to the students and giving them their own playground to explore technology and to apply it to their own interests.

CFY has followed a similar strategy, enlisting the support of families and bringing them together around the computer console. New York City's chancellor of schools, Joe Klein, has praised their efforts, noting that computers are the most underused assets in terms of educating our children. Programs like CFY, he says, "are setting us on the right track."

The organization is emerging as a leader in green technology as well. Tens of millions of computer monitors are discarded every year, and cathode ray tubes pose an increasing threat to the environment. *PC Magazine* recently called on its readers to recycle, and the company started forwarding used computers to CFY's home learning centers.

When we first took CFY under our wing, the organization provided home computers and educational training for more than five thousand families in New York City. Today, that number has crested well past fifteen thousand nationally. We are proud of the way we've helped this nonprofit grow.

We count CFY as one of our successes because it has a business model that will appeal to educators, community organizers, and policy makers in an economic crunch: If you want to get an immediate return on your investment, we tell them, donate a desktop to a low-income family; you'll see an instantaneous change in everyone.

CHAPTER 16

SEEDING YOUNG ENTREPRENEURS

Nobody talks about entrepreneurship as survival, but that's exactly what it is and what nurtures creative thinking.

Anita Roddick

AS WE CONTINUED OUR SEARCH for programs that were helping low-income youth, we heard about a visionary named Steve Mariotti at the National Foundation for Teaching Entrepreneurship (NFTE). Because this organization was focusing on creativity and self-sufficiency, it mirrored the values of ThinkQuest, with one big difference: It was showing teenagers how to launch businesses, not websites. In spring 2005, we made a cold call to Mariotti, who eagerly explained his mission.

In the 1980s, Mariotti left the corporate world for the classroom and started teaching math to at-risk kids in Bedford-Stuyvesant in Brooklyn and "Fort Apache" in the South Bronx. Fidgety and ill at ease, the students turned every opportunity to learn into a discipline problem. Day after day, they taunted Mariotti, hoping to divert him from the math lessons they had failed to master.

In desperation, Mariotti took off his wristwatch, held it up in front of the class, and asked: "How much do you think it cost to make this? And how much could you sell it for?" Suddenly the classroom came alive, and the kids started calculating markups and percentages. By teaching real-world scenarios and focusing on economic survival, Mariotti realized, he could teach important skills: basic math and long-term planning.

A MAN AND HIS VISION

Over the next year, Mariotti developed a course for urban entrepreneurs and watched students tagged as potential dropouts turn into "entrepreneurial geysers." In 1989, he put these principles into action on a larger stage, creating the National Foundation for Teaching Entrepreneurship.

Says Mariotti, at-risk teens have a natural business sense, and they also have different personality traits from traditional learners. "These students want to go out and make things happen. In a classroom, they are supposed to be quiet and reserved. That's why the traditional approach to teaching doesn't work."

Mariotti knew that asking these teens to copy down dry lectures and dull equations was a recipe for disaster. Something had to be done to capture their imagination and to give them marketable skills before they went out into the world. Otherwise, they'd be stuck in low-paying jobs and unable to care for their families and themselves.

Poverty results when people undersell themselves for a low hourly wage, Mariotti explained. "I tell kids, 'It's not enough to support yourself. If you own something, you can sell it to others for a multiple of what you paid for it. That's the beauty of business ownership. And that's a way for you to get ahead.'

"There are a billion young people living below the poverty line," Mariotti told us. "NFTE uses business to engage low-income students academically and to teach them that they are potential stakeholders in the American dream. We'd love to have your help."

Entrepreneurship education gives young people a stake in developing their own communities, he added. "We've made the mistake of thinking that this knowledge is only for adults and should be taught in business schools. That's way too late. If we really want to change society from the ground up, we need to start teaching kids about balance sheets and compound earnings beginning in grade school."

We asked Mariotti if all kids would respond to this kind of program. About one in five at-risk kids have a natural feel for business, he said. But the personality traits of a successful entrepreneur—a positive attitude, a tolerance for stress and failure—can be developed with the proper nurturing. "Markets are full of ambiguity," he said. "Young people can be taught to understand this and to work with it."

We thought this was an intriguing answer. The goal of twenty-first-century education, we believed, was to prepare young people for a world characterized by increasing volatility and uncertainty. According to the U.S. Department of Labor, young people entering the workforce today can expect to change jobs at least eight or nine times before they retire. Boston career consultant and author of *Rethinking Work* Cliff Hakim warns, "Even if you work for a big company, you will need to cope with constant change. Every worker has to have an entrepreneurial mind-set."[19]

Those of us in the high-tech field had learned this lesson well. We'd already witnessed large-scale economic shifts as the Internet allowed us to tap markets and labor in distant parts of the world. There will be more radical changes ahead as we explore new energy alternatives and begin to reframe the American economy.

ANS JOINS IN

We wanted to make the disadvantaged part of the solution. It seemed obvious that the path out of poverty had to involve teaching kids how to make money!

HOW KIDS LEARN ABOUT MONEY

The 2000 best seller *Rich Dad, Poor Dad* noted that upper-income kids had the advantage because they'd learned, in more informal settings, how the system works. Rich kids get a sense of the market economy at the dinner table listening to Dad talk about his investments, researchers said, while poor kids listen to Dad talk about problems with his boss or making ends meet. In short, the most important conversation about money takes place at home, and kids from low-income families never get to hear those conversations about how to make money grow.

While most vocational education programs focus on improving a young person's labor or productivity by a small margin, the National Foundation for Teaching Entrepreneurship (NFTE) aims a lot higher. It shows kids that they can own the output of their labor, teaching them how to think about and create wealth and giving them ways to practice their business skills, just like they'd practice basketball or soccer.

"Talking to young people about markets, selling, income statements, long-range planning, and resources is terribly important," says NFTE founder Steve Mariotti. "This helps them understand the basic concepts of debt and equity." When he first launched the program, he recalls, "students were amazed to find out that $1,000 a year can grow into more than $250,000 over fifty years, with interest compounding yearly at 12 percent." Of course, interest rates have changed. But Mariotti's argument underscores the point that there is more to getting ahead than working for an hourly wage.

In 2005, ANS provided a multiyear grant of more than $500,000 to help NFTE set up an office in Miami-Dade County, an area with one of the highest dropout rates in the nation, yet one of the strongest entrepreneurial sectors in the United States. Ninety percent of companies in the Miami–Fort Lauderdale market had twenty employees or fewer, making this a hotbed for small businesses, according to the Small Business Association. The NFTE program would allow us to channel low-income students directly into an active local economy.

Our choice to lead this initiative was Alice Horn, a clothing designer who had founded Kid Ventures in 1999, teaching entrepreneurship to middle-schoolers through use of the arts. Students in thirteen schools throughout South Florida were creating greeting cards and coffee mugs and selling them to banks and local businesses. Horn had also developed a grade-school curriculum to teach product development, pricing, and marketing. Within six years, several of these student businesses had moved into malls and attracted a larger client base. Horn merged Kid Ventures with NFTE South Florida and then designed a curriculum to teach business skills in grades 6 through 12.

"Our program in South Florida is unique," she says, "because it has the longest reach. Our program starts in middle school, then goes straight through high school. NFTE is now looking to replicate this model across the country."

In January 2006, Rudy Crew, the superintendent of the Miami-Dade public school system, welcomed the NFTE training into the classrooms and added to the ANS grant. Students in South Florida now have six years in which to develop entrepreneurial skills and experiment with business plans.

We supported a comprehensive program in entrepreneurship education that includes:

- Computer games to teach negotiation, planning, and problem-solving skills;
- Wholesale field trips and business expos to show students how to negotiate directly with vendors;
- A Summer Entrepreneurial Leadership Academy to prepare students and teachers from local schools to participate in a business expo;
- An Advanced Technology Business Camp to teach NFTE alumni advanced business strategies and technology-based marketing tools;

- NFTE University, a program to train local teachers in the entrepreneurship curriculum;
- Ongoing technical assistance to teachers and administrator for business classes and field trips; and
- Competitions from the local to the national level. (School-wide contests feed promising students into a local competition sponsored by NFTE South Florida. Winners go on to the NFTE regional competition sponsored by Merrill Lynch. Students with the best business plans then enter the national finals sponsored by Smith Barney in New York.)

Within the first year, NFTE South Florida established partnerships with dozens of local businesses and was awarded a $130,000 contract by the local school board. Soon the program attracted corporate donors like Royal Caribbean, American Express, Washington Mutual, and Staples. In a very short time, we had achieved our goal—making the NFTE program financially independent. Crew called NFTE "the centerpiece of the regional economy."

NFTE helps kids believe in themselves, all the while teaching them how to collaborate and problem solve, gather information, and adapt to a changing marketplace. Under the direction of Horn, the NFTE South Florida program has become the largest and most successful in the country.

A WIDE RANGE OF BENEFITS

While NFTE's goal is to make young people economically independent, we were pleased to find that there were academic benefits to entrepreneurship training as well. A study by Harvard's Graduate School of Education showed that NFTE grads' interest in attending college increased by 32 percent, and their occupational aspirations (a sense of what they could achieve in life) increased by 44 percent. In addition, they were more likely to engage in independent reading. Teachers also reported that NFTE students were more attentive in class. "This program seems to be working. I no longer have to fight with iPods, cell phones, and apathy," one high school teacher said.

According to the Bill and Melinda Gates Foundation, lack of engagement is "the main overriding reason" kids are dropping out of school. Yet NFTE kids are completely absorbed by their classes. Once they get the "business bug," they are also more likely to do well in standard subjects like English and math.

Jump-Starting Careers

Many NFTE students have turned hobbies into successful businesses. Teenager Eric Mund noticed that his family's photographic history might be lost because the media they were stored on had become obsolete. In his spare time, Eric began converting the family slides, snapshots, and videos to a digital source, adding music and narration. Then he started performing the same service for neighbors and friends. This led to the creation of a company, Digital Video Express. In 2008, Eric's business plan won the NFTE regional competition.

Though NFTE awards are generally given to individuals, in 2008, four teenage girls from Miami, who call themselves "Les Dames du Chocolat," won the regional competition. These young women formed a partnership and turned their passion for sweets into a thriving enterprise.

"We took all our students on a wholesale buying trip," says Horn. "And while other kids were buying T-shirts and knickknacks for resale, the girls pooled their money and bought an enormous chocolate fountain. They are now catering parties, offering fresh fruit dipped in chocolate, and their events have been featured in the *Miami Herald*." Les Dames du Chocolat has a promotional CD and a MySpace page where clients blog about their products. All four seniors are headed for college or culinary school, but they plan to keep up their chocolate business and hope to take their product all over the world.

Breaking the Cycle of Poverty

Equally important, NFTE has been a lifeline for many students, seeing them through personal and financial hardships. In his sophomore year of high school, for example, Juan Carlos Quinones was turned out of the house by his parents. An NFTE teacher helped him find an apartment and a job. In class, he started a business called Hang It, selling portable purse hooks, and he was soon able to support himself. Juan bought the hardware from a company in New York and then began to market his product to restaurants and beauty salons. "Why should your customers put a $300 purse on the floor," he asked, "when they can hook it on the side of a table?"

This enterprising young man won an award in the NFTE's national competition, and after graduation, he began working in an accounting firm. Juan continues to make $6,000 a year from his home business; he is the sole distributor of purse hooks in the state of Florida.

"With the combined income from his business and his job, Juan has been living independently since age 16," says NFTE director Horn. "Once at risk for being homeless, he's now enrolled part-time at Miami-Dade College. NFTE showed him there were alternatives and gave him a way to support himself in times of dire need."

Seeding Student Businesses

In 2008 alone, NFTE South Florida produced twenty-one hundred young entrepreneurs. ANS decided to give the most promising ones some venture capital to get their businesses off the ground. We put up the seed funds for the Entrepreneurship Club, which now provides its members with a $500 stipend to launch a website, purchase inventory or supplies and materials, and promote a fledgling business. The E-Club also provides hands-on help. Local business executives serve as mentors, showing students how to become licensed in the state of Florida, open bank accounts, and prepare their marketing strategies. As part of the program, the students design their own commercials and brochures.

Doris Bakana, a student at North Miami Beach Senior High School, was a shy, retiring young man who faced many challenges when he first started the NFTE training. He shared a room with his mother in another family's apartment, and he had to take several buses to participate in the NFTE classes. He wasn't sure what he could make of his life. But by listening to motivational tapes and videos at the library when his spirits were down, he forged ahead and devoted all his energy to a start-up: Speedy Cleaning, providing janitorial services for offices and homes. Doris went on to win the NFTE regional business competition and to join the E-Club. He received $500 in start-up funds and now has several clients.

After making NFTE the organizing factor in his life, Doris grew more outgoing and confident. He now hopes to launch a second business: an inspirational speakers' bureau to help other young people follow their dreams.

It's hard to capture in statistics what is often best expressed in heartfelt statements by NFTE students and teachers. At Doris's award ceremony, his teacher Kim Davenport thanked us for bringing NFTE to her school, saying, "You give our students hope."

According to a recent study of NFTE graduates, three-quarters view starting a small business as a realistic way out of poverty.

A New Era for Hispanic Enterprises

In the Miami-Dade area, NFTE students are also joining the growing ranks of businesses owned and operated by Hispanics. There are now two million such businesses in the United States, generating close to

$300 billion in revenues each year, according to the Small Business Administration. The number of these businesses is expected to grow to 3.2 million by 2010, contributing $465 billion to the economy. The Census Bureau projects that the Hispanic population will grow to fifty million by 2010, and *Hispanic Business* magazine estimates they will have a purchasing power of $1 trillion. NFTE alumni will be in the vanguard of this growing market.

Today, Miami's Florida International University produces the largest number of Hispanic business majors in the country. "NFTE expects to contribute more students to this program in the years ahead," says Horn. "From the start, all of our courses have been offered in Spanish as well as English, so we could be part of this emerging trend."

THE RISE OF TEEN ENTREPRENEURS

In the current economic environment, teen entrepreneurs embody hope for the future, and we are pleased to have contributed to this trend. As a result of programs like NFTE, administrators are starting to think more seriously about teaching entrepreneurship in our public schools. In 2007, the Aspen Institute's Youth Entrepreneurship Strategy Group said that every student in a federally funded high school should receive hands-on training in these skills.

Dane Linn, director of the educational division of the National Governors Association, notes that U.S. schools lag behind other nations in competitiveness, and we need to focus on improving student readiness for work and life. He notes that entrepreneurship education helps students build a portfolio of competencies.

"Congress should amend that law to fund the certification of high school educators to teach [these skills] to students most likely to be left behind," adds Michael Caslin, NFTE's executive vice president for public policy.

To date, NFTE has trained more than forty-eight hundred teachers in thirty-one states and thirteen countries. Teachers can become certified with thirty-two hours of training during the school year and four days in the summer months. This is yet another example of how nonprofit organizations can help our educational system change and keep up with the times.

Other countries have begun to stress entrepreneurship education. The United Kingdom, Ireland, and Germany are in the forefront, while in China and India, interest in entrepreneurship classes is exploding. NFTE's experiment in Miami-Dade County, with ANS financial backing, has shown that teaching entrepreneurship in our public schools is both a good way to help students earn money for college and to stimulate the regional economy.

Building Self-Reliance

As we supported NFTE, we also learned that young people today are following a different pathway to success. While their grandparents' generation looked for security and stability within the corporation, most students feel they can count only on themselves. According to the Institute for the Future (IFTF), an independent research group in California, we're about to see the most entrepreneurial generation ever. IFTF, which has forecasted emerging trends in the global marketplace for nearly forty years, says that Generation Yers don't plan to work for corporations. Instead, they want go out on their own and launch small businesses.[20]

"They view traditional big company jobs as constraining and unstable. They have a clear wish to be the captains of their own destiny, and they see entrepreneurship as a way of maintaining independence," says the IFTF report. Generation Yers also have several traits that will help them to be successful entrepreneurs. As a group, they are:

- Ready to take risks and try new things;
- Tolerant of trial and error, and prepared to learn from their mistakes;
- Strong on conceptual thinking, able to build on their ideas and adapt them as required; and
- Able to envision a wide range of outcomes. Having grown up with scenario-based video games and interactive media, they know there is more than one result, and that this changes depending on their strategy.

"Proving the relevance of knowledge becomes an important factor when trying to engage these students," says IFTF. Technology and entrepreneurship both will play a larger role.

IFTF also notes that economic growth in the years ahead is likely to come from what it calls "accidental entrepreneurs." Of the 26 million businesses currently operating in the United States, 20 million are sole proprietorships that are run by freelancers or hobbyists.

NFTE is a major contributor to this new economic stream. According to the Koch Foundation, participation in the NFTE program has increased small-business formation rates by 45 percent. And, 76 percent of NFTE NYC alumni think starting and owning a small business is a realistic way out of poverty, versus 46 percent of the comparison group. Minority business ownership from NFTE alumni was also four times higher than the national average for minority adults, the study notes.

ANS made important contributions by showing NFTE how to integrate new technology into their national program; how to create a blueprint for entrepreneurial education that begins in the fourth grade and continues right through high school; and how to fuel the regional economy in South Florida with its support of student businesses.

Both industry and government are beginning to understand that an entrepreneurial orientation is key to innovation, to continued economic growth, and to the creation of new jobs. While struggling parents used to tell their teens to "get a job," today they might say "start a business" as a way of helping out.

NFTE South Florida helped make the case that entrepreneurship training can change the lives of teenagers and strengthen the regional economy. Our initial investment of $500,000 was immediately matched by the Miami-Dade school system and corporations. Within a year, the project was completely self-sufficient, and so were many of the student enterprises we supported.

CHAPTER 17

NEW OPPORTUNITIES FOR LOW-INCOME YOUTH

There is a wonderful mythical law of nature that the three things we crave most in life—happiness, freedom, and peace of mind—are always attained by giving them to someone else.

Peyton Conway March

IN SPRING 2006, our contacts at New Profit, a venture philanthropy organization specializing in social programs, were eager to tell us about a high-tech entrepreneur who was helping low-income youth find jobs in the critical years right after high school graduation. A few weeks later, we met Gerald Chertavian and learned that too many young people end up unemployed or in dead-end jobs.

Access to higher education and opportunity for advancement have always been the basic elements of the American dream, he told us. Yet many high school graduates are now finding that dream unreachable. According to the Anne E. Casey Foundation, some 4.1 million young adults are disconnected from the mainstream economy and are likely to remain so for the rest of their lives. That foundation further reports that 15 percent of all eighteen- to twenty-five-year-olds are out of work after receiving their high school diplomas. Within the few years following their graduation, they find themselves doing menial labor, with no chance of advancement, and raising families on less than $20,000 a year.

A MAN AND HIS MISSION

Chertavian had started Year Up to give high school graduates a range of business and high-tech skills and then to place them in corporate internships. His goal was to take them from the margins into the mainstream of the U.S. economy.

While Chertavian had already established branches of Year Up in Boston and Providence, his goal was to have a national footprint by the year 2016. As he talked about his business plan, we knew right away this was a project ANS should be supporting.

Year Up is targeting very specific urban areas. "Roughly seven hundred thousand of our nation's disadvantaged youth live in thirty cities. If we have a Year Up program in every one of these," Chertavian said, "we can make a major impact." This expansion would cost $18 million, and Year Up's capital campaign was gaining steam by the time we met Chertavian.

Also attractive was the partnership Year Up had established with industry and government agencies. They were using the ANS model—that is, creating a web of alliances to achieve their goal.

On average, it costs Year Up $24,000 to move an unemployed young adult into the mainstream economy. Of that, $16,000 comes from a corporate internship, $4,000 comes from a private donor, and $4,000 from the government.

"Government agencies are used to paying $8,000 for each individual on welfare," Chertavian explained. "This is a better deal for them, and they are increasingly willing to invest in our program."

The private donors also get something back. They are eliminating poverty in their own communities by investing in continuing education for urban youth. When a Year Up student gets a job, the donor is likely to contribute again the following year. As Chertavian put it, "These people know they are investing in America's future, and they find the concept of individual sponsorship rewarding."

Year Up had one of the most elegant business models we had ever seen. The question was, How could ANS contribute? To figure that out, we immersed ourselves in the organization's history and started to get to know many of the young people whose lives it had dramatically changed.

THE INSPIRATION FOR YEAR UP

Chertavian learned the value of mentoring as a Big Brother on Manhattan's lower East Side. In 1987, he walked into a housing project at 54-64 Rutgers Street, the most heavily photographed crime scene in the city. The walk was littered with needles and broken bottles. Yet Chertavian found a spark of promise in this worn-down neighborhood: David Heredia was an energetic ten-year-old boy, with a loving mother and a gift for drawing.

"He was bright and enthusiastic," Chertavian said. "The only thing against him was that he was born on the wrong side of the opportunity divide."

Chertavian, in stumbling Spanish, told David's mother that he would take care of her son every Saturday for the next three years. In that time, he saw firsthand the problems facing urban youth. He learned how talented they were and how few opportunities they had to develop their talents.

Chertavian introduced David to new environments, stretching the boy beyond his comfort zone. "The first time I brought him to my home on Long Island, he said it was too quiet and too dark, that the windows opened out onto the grass, and anyone could crawl right in," he recalled. "Years later, David told me how much he hated me for introducing him to so many white people."

At fourteen, David decided he wanted to go to college and study animation. Chertavian, then working at Chemical Bank, decided to invest in the boy's future. He offered to pay the tuition if David got accepted and kept up a good average. Now thirty-two, David has his own design company in Los Angeles and has recently become a Big Brother to continue the tradition of "giving back."

There were many gifted young people like David who needed some help to realize their potential. In 1990, Chertavian left Chemical Bank and applied to Harvard Business School, hoping to design a national program for inner-city youth.

On his Harvard application, he noted, "Young, talented minds are being wasted and unless an effort is made to provide a logical, well-organized framework for these individuals to pursue their aspirations, a Third World will develop within our own country." While pursuing his MBA, Chertavian came up with a plan to prepare young people for the workforce, find them entry-level jobs within the corporate world, and encourage them to keep on learning through college courses and career workshops.

First, he followed Peter Drucker's advice—"To do good, you have to do well"—founding a high-tech consulting company in London that posted earnings of $20 million a year. In 1999, Chertavian sold the company and came back to his native state of Massachusetts to lay the groundwork for Year Up.

Entrepreneur Craig Underwood provided introductions to senior management at Digitas, Putnam Investments, and Bain and Company. Chertavian explained to them how he was going to help disadvantaged kids and, at the same time, build the local labor force. Underwood later confessed, "When Gerald started talking, I had no idea whether he could deliver."

His presentation, however, was not only passionate and idealistic—"Here's an opportunity to help urban youth"—but also oriented toward the bottom line. The cost of a "wrong hire" at entry level could be as high as $18,000, but Year Up would provide workers who were well trained and highly motivated, reducing the attrition rate. The companies signed on, and Tim Dibble, founding member of Alta Communications, a venture capital firm, offered his company headquarters as a base.

Chertavian began focusing his training program on the desktop skills much needed by the health-care and financial industries. Partner's Health Care System, State Street Bank, Merrill Lynch, and Bank of America were among the first to offer apprenticeships to Year Up participants, and soon the word spread: These young people had the latest tech skills, and they were courteous and competent. This nonprofit was a terrific source of highly motivated employees.

"Our candidates fill out a very long application form, with a personal essay indicating their level of commitment to the program," Chertavian told us. "Our classroom work then focuses on computer skills, oral and written communication, email etiquette, public speaking, and how to craft a resume."

Year Up students earn eighteen college credits through Pace College in New York, Cambridge College in Massachusetts, and other academic partners. They also receive a monthly stipend to cover their living expenses throughout the training period.

Trainees spend the first six months learning basic skills, then they spend a second six months working as apprentices with Year Up's corporate partners. By graduation, they have marketable career skills worth in the neighborhood of $30,000-plus a year.

ANS was also intrigued by Year Up's reputation for tough love. Before training, students sign a contract promising to uphold certain basic values, such as promptness and respect for their employers. They are also expected to dress professionally, turn all work assignments in on time, and treat others with courtesy.

"We don't have that soft tributary of lower expectations that often creeps into our social services sector—'How can I ask people to be on time if they have problems at home?'" Chertavian said. "If you dumb the program down, that's the most disrespectful thing that you can do."

In addition to accountability, Year Up teaches team building and relationships. Students learn how to shake hands, look other people in the eye, and be fully present when they engage with others. Multitasking is viewed as a distraction. The emphasis is on giving clients and coworkers your full attention. The result is that Year Up grads hone their concentration and learn a kind of receptive listening that is valued in the corporate world.

On our first site visit, several Year Up trainees approached us asking: "Is there anything I can do to help you? Can I tell you more about our work?" They were perfect ambassadors for the program— outgoing, confident, and willing to show me what they'd learned.

When we asked how Year Up managed to turn recent high school grads into such extraordinary employees, Chertavian replied, "With a culture of high expectations and high support. Year Up has no separate cubicles or offices. The staff work in a bullpen, so each moment becomes a teaching opportunity. Trainees watch as their coaches conduct conference calls and hold meetings. And we have regular Friday feedback sessions where students learn how to give and receive constructive criticism."

WHO BENEFITS?

Meeting Year Up students reminded us of the days we spent running ThinkQuest and dealing with students from so many other cultures. Of Year Up's recent graduates, 55 percent are African American, 35 percent are Hispanic, and 10 percent are immigrants from Eastern Europe. Many come from the world's trouble spots, like Chechnya, Bosnia, Kazakhstan, and North Africa.

Immigrants and racial minorities are the fastest-growing groups in the United States, Chertavian told us, and they're getting the least amount of education at a time when our knowledge-based economy is demanding higher-level skills. "Year Up was founded to address the opportunity divide between those who can get into the game and those who can't."

Over several months, we met many of the young people Year Up had helped launch. Fred el Pena, one of the first to graduate from Year Up's training program, emigrated from El Salvador. He was hired by Fidelity's Center for Applied Technology in Boston and is the first person in his family to own a home.

Ousdane Chadic, who arrived from Haiti at age sixteen, graduated from one of Boston's public high schools. To get a job, she knew she had to improve her communication skills. The trouble was, she needed to start earning money. Year Up provided her with a basic wage while she practiced public speaking and began to build her confidence. "I'm better at this now," she says. "And some of the things we've learned here, we wouldn't have learned even if we were at college."

At twenty, Roberto Velez worked nights cleaning jets at JFK Airport. The job was hard, there was no possibility of advancement, and he didn't have the time or money to learn new skills. After graduating from Year Up, he landed an internship on Wall Street, and by age twenty-three, he was making four times his previous salary. This well-groomed young man told *Success* magazine: "My grandmother, she doesn't speak much English. I haven't seen my mother for about twenty years, and my father has been in and out of the criminal environment. I basically came from nothing to something." Roberto now serves as a role model for other young people in his community.

After talking with scores of Year Up trainees, we heard from the companies that hired them. Nine out of ten employers said that Year Up grads have either met or exceeded their expectations. We also learned that 65 percent of their trainees go on to pursue a college education and increase their value in the workforce.

Reversing the Downward Spiral

According to the U.S. government, 4.3 million young people are now condemned to live in poverty. But Chertavian told us that that figure may be higher, and his goal is to reverse it.

"The government sets the minimum living wage for a family of four at $19,200, but this figure is based on food costs and doesn't factor in the recent increases in housing and rent. The real poverty cutoff should be $38,000. Below that level, people can't afford proper health care or nutrition, they can't save, and they can't afford entertainment—not movies or an occasional ball game—or the most basic personal hygiene. There are some pretty stark choices they have to make."

After Year Up graduates learn the basics of business and technology, however, they immediately increase their earning power as well as their likelihood of promotion. On average, they earn $15 an hour, or $32,000 a year.

There are advantages for the taxpayer as well, Chertavian points out. As these young people make their way into the mainstream, they need fewer unemployment benefits and social services—a win-win situation for the whole community.

THE POWER OF NETWORKING

Within a month of our first meeting, we were sold on Year Up and asked Chertavian for a proposal to make this organization more effective. We made a few changes to his plan and provided Year Up with a $500,000 grant to build "The Life After Year Up" program. Within two years, Year Up would have more than ten thousand graduates. ANS proposed to create alumni centers across the country to provide opportunities for advanced training, as well as a forum for sharing job contacts. Our goal was to give low-income youth the same kind of networking opportunities as students who had attended Harvard or MIT had.

Year Up grads are increasingly isolated as they move into the corporate world. They tend to leave the old neighborhood as soon as they have better-paying jobs, and many find that they are the first people of color to be hired by tech or customer service departments. It was critically important, therefore, that they had a place to meet and mentor one another.

Year Up alumni also needed to build their professional contacts. "Studies show that eight out of ten job interviews come from a personal referral or network," Chertavian had told us. "That means Year Up students are essentially competing for the two jobs that are left. One of the biggest problems for low-income people is: How do you find the people who will get you an interview? How do you find a way in?"

As pioneers in the high-tech world, we understood the value of a strong professional network. We also knew that the alumni centers would keep these careers in motion. Yet this effort to serve Year Up grads had other, more immediate benefits. Most important, it attracted a $10 million commitment from Microsoft to provide computer training to all Year Up trainees. For a very small investment, we were able to attract a larger donor and help the organization as a whole. "Thanks to the ANS investment," Chertavian said, "all Year Up grads receive online certification from Microsoft. The creation of a national alumni center has had a ripple effect for our students, like Vista and Head Start."

In the past two years, we have watched Year Up alumni develop a strong commitment to giving back. Rashawn Facey-Castillo, who apprenticed at an investment company and then moved to State Street Bank, is one of the few black men to succeed in the financial industry. In April 2006, he started a mentorship program called MOVEMENT at his local YMCA, teaching young people how to avoid street gangs, pursue their dreams, and serve as positive role models for their peers. Facey-Castillo's group reaches out to other members of the community and changes the stereotypical view of inner-city youth.

Abdul Tijani survived the civil war in Sierra Leone and then came to the United States and enrolled in Year Up. While finishing his corporate apprenticeship, he was the victim of a random shooting. After receiving a prosthetic leg, Tijani completed his training and secured a position at the headquarters for Stop and Shop. Tijani presents an award each year to the Year Up student who has had to overcome the greatest odds, and he serves as a model of personal courage.

These are the kind of committed young people who will continue to reach out and inspire others.

Year Up's alumni association continues to grow and has recently attracted some high-powered talent from the ranks of retired executives. A single African American mom in her twenties, for instance, is now learning how to run a board meeting from a Harvard Business School graduate in his seventies, and the association is emerging as a pioneer in intergenerational learning as well.

FROM CORPORATE LADDER TO CORPORATE LATTICE

When I started out at IBM in 1960, I had had three years of college and one computer course at the University of Kansas. Most of my learning was on the job, and I found myself moving on every three years. The formula went like this: The first year, I'd learn the job and who to trust; the second year, I'd take the results on the road; and the third year, new windows of opportunities would open and I'd find another challenge. Back then, this pattern was unusual. Today, it is the norm for every young person entering the workforce.

Working on the bleeding edge of technology, I also observed that creativity takes the zigzag path more often than it moves in a straight line. This is now true not just for engineers and inventors but also for nearly every industry in America. As the trajectory of success is governed more and more by innovation, there is no vertical climb. A recent study by Cathleen Benko, published by Harvard Business School, shows that aspiring young executives don't scale the corporate ladder anymore.[21] Instead, they spend a lot of time moving sideways and navigating what's referred to as the "corporate lattice," taking jobs in different departments, making lateral moves to gain new expertise. It's only by taking a side step, Benko says, that workers build new skills.

Year Up is a model of twenty-first-century education because it first provides an entree into the workforce and then serves as a lifelong resource, helping graduates stay ahead of the innovation curve. There's an old adage, "Teach a person how to fish and he won't bother you for a couple of days." After the Internet emerged, we said, "Teach someone how to use and learn on the Web, and they won't bother you for weeks." Now we add social networking into the mix and say, "Teach people how to build strong relationships, and they'll have the tools they need to succeed in life."

A NEW MOVEMENT FOR SOCIAL CHANGE

Year Up has given us a big return for a small investment. Its alumni association now has a welcoming presence in five major cities. Alumni form their own counsels, elect representatives, and organize their own events. One group teaches elderly residents in their community how to use Microsoft tools. Another group mentors high school students. Their message is: If you want to succeed, you need to surround yourself with positive influences.

With ten thousand Year Up alumni giving back to the community, we will see a strong impetus for social change. Young people from the inner cities will recognize Year Up alumni as role models and, in turn, begin to mentor others. As more of them succeed, we will reach a tipping point.

By 2010, Year Up will serve young adults in five cities: Boston, Providence, New York, Washington, and San Francisco. Plans are under way to open branches in Chicago and Dallas as well.

NO MORE PARTIAL SOLUTIONS

ANS backed Year Up because it has outstanding leadership, a financial structure built for growth, and the means to impact the lives of its trainees, their families, and their communities. In short, it met all the criteria ANS has set for responsible giving.

As engineers of the Internet, we learned not to trust partial solutions but to consider every aspect of a problem. As we moved into the field of philanthropy, we held on to this 360-degree vision.

We chose to invest a good deal of time and energy just figuring out how we could help Year Up because it was an organization with a comprehensive focus. It looked at youth development, college access, and workforce placement, while other programs tended to force kids down a single path.

Low-income teenagers who have just graduated from high school have no money, no way of supporting themselves. They are also still in the process of maturing, finding out who they are. They need to start building a sense of self-empowerment and self-confidence, so we liked Year Up's emphasis on self-development.

Next there is the problem of higher education. Young adults with a four-year college degree start off earning 25 percent more than those who have just a high school diploma. It would be ideal if all students could go to college full-time, but in our country, only a small

A NEW BREED OF SOCIAL ENTREPRENEUR

The antipoverty movement in America has changed considerably in the past thirty years because more talented entrepreneurs are willing to work in the social sector. Year Up's founder, Gerald Chertavian, and two of its regional directors have a Harvard MBA, and another is a Rhodes scholar—an indication that high achievers in the forty-something age group are drawn to the business of helping others. Nearly twenty years ago, only a few of the students at Harvard Business School were interested in human services. Today, the most popular extracurricular activity is the Social Enterprise Club.

While Year Up regional directors have impressive pedigrees, they also know how to talk to kids from low-income communities. Says Chertavian, "Our staff is 45 percent people of color, and we all know what it's like to grow up in tough neighborhoods."

Jay Banfield, who directs the Year Up office in San Francisco, was raised on public assistance, got his MBA at Berkeley, then went to work at Oracle. "Growing up, I had to dress in front of an open stove because there was no heat in the house. Yet there were people who looked out for me," he said, "and gave me an opportunity to get ahead. I joined Year Up because I believe our society has an obligation to look out for young people with talent and help them use their gifts—especially in today's volatile economy."

minority can afford to. "For every hundred Americans between the age of eighteen and twenty-four, only eight go straight through college," Chertavian told us. "The rest drop out, work for a while, then return to finish their degrees."

We liked the fact that Year Up placed its trainers in corporate jobs that allowed them to earn a livable wage in thirty or forty hours a week and to pursue higher education at night.

Education policy makers are in the privileged minority that has gone straight through college. Perhaps that's why they have yet to design programs that serve the other 92 percent of young adults who can't afford a private college at $40,000 a year. They need to consider, however, that programs like Year Up may be the only realistic approach.

Year Up's emphasis on workforce development also appealed to us because we saw the link between providing jobs and building a strong national economy. As Chertavian said, "Writing off 50 percent of those young people who aren't going to college is morally wrong. It's also detrimental to our national competitiveness. Human capital will be a core asset in the economy of the twenty-first century, and we can't afford to waste this precious resource."

In the long run, Year Up and ANS had the same goals: to use technology as a lever for economic change, and to be sure that nobody gets left out.

A SUSTAINABLE BUSINESS MODEL

Year Up has one of the most elegant business plans we've ever seen. Here's the formula that allows them to make every new regional office self-sufficient.

Corporate IT departments pay $775 a week for each intern. This income is used to underwrite the first six months of training and to pay each student a stipend of $180 to $250 per week. That means the students earn a living wage while they're learning, and the program can be replicated in other cities with minimum start-up costs. Corporate partners pay the lion's share of operating expenses, yet Year Up has also raised more than $16 million in growth capital to set up shop in thirty target cities.

By applying sound business principles, Chertavian has begun to solve what policy makers have long considered an intractable problem: finding gainful employment for low-income youth. In 2008, *Fast Company* magazine and the Monitor Group, a global consulting firm, cited Chertavian as one of the nation's top social entrepreneurs. "This year we've seen an explosion of experiments, many of them engineered by one-time Wall Street heavies, that attempt to bring new capital—and capital-market dynamics—to the realm of social good," wrote *Fast Company* contributor Keith Hammond. "Through these deals, social entrepreneurs and businesses are raising the stakes, and changing old-style capitalism as we know it."

A NEW MODEL FOR SOCIAL SERVICES

In the 1960s and 1970s, nonprofits provided most of our social services, but now the private sector has to be involved as well. According to *New York Times* columnist David Brooks, the United States needs a new social contract, one that requires business to invest in the public good. The State Street Corporation in Boston has just committed $5.4 million to hire and train Year Up apprentices over the next three years. This is just one way companies can invest in human capital and, at the same time, help transform our cities.

Partnerships like this are going to be the wave of the future. "This isn't the laissez-faire social contract of the 19th century," Brooks writes, "but neither is it the centralized, big bureaucracy contract of the 20th century. It's a contract that envisions society as a dense but flexible web of social networks."

This is exactly the approach ANS took to help build the information superhighway—creating a web of alliances with government, universities, research labs, and private industry.

Brooks also points out that the old employer-based social contract is eroding, and most Americans can no longer count on corporate pensions and health care to provide them with a sense of economic stability. We need a new approach to help those who fall between the cracks and a social system that fosters self-sufficiency. If people do slip and require government support, he adds, they should be induced to rebound and take care of themselves.

We agree. We supported Year Up because it creates a more level playing field and fosters economic independence, helping young people at the crucial age when they are first entering the workforce. We believe that programs like this are part of an emerging trend and will have a national impact.

David Gergen, a professor of public service at Harvard's John F. Kennedy School of Government and White House adviser to Presidents Nixon, Ford, Reagan, and Clinton, believes America's future will be shaped by social entrepreneurs. He has compared their efforts to the early years of the civil rights movement. "In those days," he said, "it wasn't clear who was in charge or what the program was, but people kept pushing forward, and things began to change."

At ANS, we have tried to help young people find economic security as they learn about the most exciting advances in the Information Age. We partnered with Year Up because this organization has the same mission. "It's wrong that our young people fail based on the color of their skin, their ZIP codes, and the bank balance of their parents," Chertavian told us in one of our first meetings. "This has led to a serious stagnation in American society. Economic mobility is now higher in European countries than it is here in the United States, and the present generation is the first to lose ground economically and fail to do better than their parents."

This is a reversal of the American dream and of the values that foster risk and innovation. By supporting projects like Year Up—as well as Computers for Youth, the National Foundation for Teaching Entrepreneurship, and the thirty other organizations that it has been our pleasure to help—we have been able to restore that dream. We have been able to give young people from all backgrounds a chance to improve themselves and to achieve a better quality of life.

PART FIVE

Guidance for Giving Back

CHAPTER 18

OUR PHILOSOPHY OF GIVING

We make a living by what we get, but we make a life by what we give.
Winston Churchill

WHEN THE INTERNET BECAME ubiquitous in the 1990s, futurist Peter Russell compared it to a *global brain*, predicting that technology would give us the collective power to address such large-scale problems as poverty, hunger, and a deteriorating environment. In the decades to come, he said, the Internet could deepen our sense of compassion and social responsibility. Emerging technologies would allow us "to form new associations, synthesize information, and perhaps solve problems presented to it," he wrote. "Then we will no longer perceive ourselves as isolated individuals; we will know ourselves to be a part of a rapidly integrating global network, the nerve cells of an awakening global brain."

We have yet to achieve this optimistic vision, chiefly because it takes human values and behavior time to catch up with technology. Yet from the start, ANS has embraced something of this wider vision, linking advances in technology to the common good.

When we helped build the information superhighway, we made sure to funnel any commercial profits back into the network, to build a national resource that would benefit all users. We created new tools to measure the performance of the Internet and helped design the next generation network that now serves our universities and research labs. Next we created a global Olympics on the Web to teach twenty-first-century skills and introduce the next generation to the magic of technology. We also designed the classroom of the future, combining three-dimensional computer models and virtual reality. Finally, we helped more than thirty other nonprofits close the opportunity gap by bringing disadvantaged youth into the mainstream economy.

The interesting thing is how such a small nonprofit managed to achieve so much. The answer lies in the fact that we were always more interested in innovation than we were in self-perpetuation.

When the market for Internet services shifted, we sold our technology to AOL and moved into the field of global education. After launching ThinkQuest, we became philanthropists, looking for other ways we could give back. Yet we didn't set out to create a big foundation. As board member McGroddy said in 2004: "Our goal should be to make a difference and then close the shop. Let's give our expertise and contacts, and use up all the money, before the passion dies." We will have done exactly that, allocating our remaining funds to worthy programs as this book goes to press in the second half of 2009.

THE KEY TO ANS'S DIFFERENCE

I'm often asked, How was ANS any different from the high-tech companies that made their money in the dot-com boom? The answer is that giving back was our mission from the very start.

According to psychologist Steven Goldbart, founder of the Money, Meaning, and Choices Institute, many dot-com millionaires suffered from "Sudden Wealth Syndrome" and had no idea what to do with their assets. But from the start, ANS was concerned with giving back. The reason: It was run by people who had reached what Erik Erikson called "the age of generativity" and who were more concerned with mentoring than they were with making money.

I started the company in my fifties, after building the first pan-European computer network for IBM and serving as vice president for the division that produced some of the world's largest supercomputers. I had achieved enough "firsts" and was now at the age of mentoring, when it's appropriate to start thinking about what kind of world we want to leave our youth. My colleagues had also reached the same turning point after long and distinguished careers. Bob Harris was near retirement after serving as controller of the IBM Credit Corporation; Jim Parker had served as CEO of Kaiser Industries, then senior vice president and chief counsel of CBS. Our board members all held senior positions in technology, publishing, and scientific research. When we asked, "How do we want this company to be remembered?" the answer wasn't for a certain high-tech patent or invention but for the gift of changing lives.

Throughout the years, our guidelines for giving have been simple:

- Focus, focus, focus—choose the "specific" area where you can make a difference.
- Use not only your cash but also your energy and contacts. Be proactive and discover what an organization needs to move to the next step.
- Don't give for incremental change; make every dollar you give count and contribute to the bigger picture.
- Help attract other funders to leverage your investment.
- Keep your eye on the projects you support and demand that they produce; you can expect what you inspect.

These guidelines have served us well and enabled us to support a wide range of ventures. But there's one more reason for our success. We saw ourselves not as experts in a given field but as agents of change. As high-tech leaders, we were used to creating a new product or service and then moving on to the next challenge. We didn't get attached to any single invention or technology. Perhaps that was why we could wear so many hats in the fields of education and philanthropy. This flexibility and openness is also what allowed us to give all our wealth away.

When asked to explain our mission, I like to tell the following story:

> A wise woman traveling in the mountains found a precious stone. The next day, she met another traveler who was hungry and opened her bag to share her food. The traveler saw the precious stone and asked the woman for it. She gave it without hesitation. The traveler left, rejoicing in his good fortune. He knew the stone would give him security for a lifetime.
>
> But, a few days later, he came back to return the stone.
>
> "I've been thinking," he said. "I know how valuable this is, but I give it back hoping you might give me something even more precious. What you have within you that enabled you to give me the stone."

ANS has always tried to promote this generosity of spirit. To support programs that would keep on giving long after we are gone. We are fortunate to have a portfolio of successes, to have helped more than thirty organizations that will continue passing on important skills to the next generation.

There is a window in time that is right for almost every program: The need is there, the leadership is there, the ideas are sustainable and useful to society. Money allowed us to be an effective catalyst and to help others grow.

Giving has long been a favorite subject for psychologists, anthropologists, economists, and marketers. Experts reaffirm the old saying that the greatest benefits accrue to the giver rather than the receiver.

The reason: Through giving, we discover how the world is made. Giving has a cosmic function, rather like the mysterious force that holds subatomic particles together. It is the glue that holds our lives and our communities together.

In *The Corporate Mystic*, Gay Hendricks and Kate Ludeman say that if you become a source of integrity, vision, and intuition, you will automatically step into a position of leadership. ANS has emerged as a leader in technology, education, and philanthropy because we have always focused on putting our core values into action. We determined early on that any venture we supported should:

1. Empower people—increase their sense of mastery and responsibility;
2. Help people learn how to learn, master change, and become more self-confident;
3. Be comprehensive and provide change makers with all the tools they need;
4. Create a strong support network that involves the private and the public spheres and reaches out to every level of society; and
5. Encourage the next generation to "pay it forward" by mentoring others and passing on the benefits they've received.

In the process, we have learned that the greatest satisfaction comes, not from holding on to wealth of any kind, but from giving all you have to others.

THE FUTURE OF GIVING IN A TOUGH ECONOMY

People have asked us if we think these values will be affected by recent and dramatic shifts in the American economy. Will social entrepreneurship take a direct hit? Will there be less money to do good and fewer people trying? We have come down on the side of cautious optimism. In the decade ahead, we are going to witness the emergence of new industries, with major innovation in the energy sector. Silicon Valley is already moving in that direction, developing new technologies to make our country green. Technology will continue to be the driver of the U.S. economy, and there will be plenty of entrepreneurs who make their money in this way and then decide to tackle social problems.

We believe social entrepreneurs will become even more important, helping us reset our priorities and reorganize our economy. In an era of change and crisis, we tend to reexamine our values and pull together for the common good. This time we will have to put our best minds to work on issues like energy independence and climate change, reforming health care, and rebuilding our failing education system. Our country will have to invest in innovation and teamwork and once again find ways of doing the impossible.

In our view, everyone is a change maker. Thanks to the Internet and new social networks, we all have the ability to make a difference in our organizations, our communities, and our countries.

Today, even grade-school kids are using the Internet to advance social causes. Last year, we funded a new program at ThinkQuest NYC to encourage students to design websites for their favorite charities. The results included, among many other noteworthy examples, Shoes4Africa and the Slate Foundation, which helps endangered species.

ThinkQuest alumni and graduates of Computers for Youth, the National Foundation for Teaching Entrepreneurship, Year Up, and the other projects we've supported are now working on new forms of collaboration and information sharing. All are helping us build communities, renew our inner cities, and close the opportunity divide.

When people ask how much a single organization can do, our answer is, "Plenty!" The ThinkQuest program alone supports 397,000 children in sixty countries, while NFTE reaches more than

230,000 students in twenty-two states and thirteen countries. By the year 2010, 700,000-plus young people from ANS-supported organizations will be serving as role models for their peers. This is the ultimate in "giving back." It's a grassroots movement enabling the next generation to build a better world, and we are proud to have made a difference in so many lives.

ACKNOWLEDGMENTS

Every project ANS has undertaken has been a collaborative effort, and there are many people to thank for helping us on our journey from scientific to social innovation. I fall on my sword now if I have left someone out, but if I have forgotten to name any of the generous individuals who helped us on our journey, it is unintentional.

With that said, I want to give special thanks to some of ANS's strongest supporters—those who have seen it through every step of its evolution. On the top of the list is my wife, Sandy, who has supported all my crazy adventures; my right arm, Kristin Mortensen, who has always told me to listen to the wise men; Jim McGroddy, who has always been available when I needed sound advice; Bob Harris, who has made sure we have never run out of cash; Linda Roberts, who pointed out so many good programs; and Larry Landweber, who contributed to almost all of our endeavors. The ANS board members deserve special thanks. They have asked the hard questions that all boards should ask and have served for almost twenty years with only a stale sandwich as their reward.

For their recollections on the early days of Internet and their early support for ANS, I am grateful to John Armstrong and Jim McGroddy, each a former senior vice president at IBM Research; Douglas Van Houweling (and his team at Merit), who is currently president and CEO of Internet2; Jordan Becker, for years second in command at ANS and now senior vice president at Science Applications International Corporation; Stephen Wolff, former director of the Division of Networking and Communications Research and Infrastructure in the National Science Foundation; Larry Landweber, former head of the Internet Society, and the John P. Morgridge Professor of Computer Science at the University of Wisconsin–Madison; Dick Liebhaber, formerly the executive vice president and CTO of MCI; Matthew Dovens and Ann O'Beay from MCI, former IBM engineers; Barry Appleman, who recently retired as the CTO of AOL; Yakov Rekhter, one of the big brains behind the growth of the Internet protocols; Bharath Kadaba, who with his IBM team built our T-3 routers, and is now the vice president of media engineering at Yahoo; Alan Baratz, our technical liaison with IBM, and now senior vice president of Network Software and System Technology Group at Cisco; my colleague Bill Schrader, who ran NYSERnet, one of the first regional networks, and later founded PSI; and John Markoff, technical writer for the *New York Times*, who not only reports the news but makes it.

I would also like to thank our European colleagues: Hagen Hultzsch, former member of the board of Deutsche Telekom, and Colin Bell, former CEO of AT&T–UK and managing director of Cable and Wireless's International Data Network Services, who both worked so hard to get the European R&D community online.

For their early efforts to bring computer education into the public schools, and their help shaping ThinkQuest, I thank Ken King, former head of the Cornell Theory Center, who helped me structure ThinkQuest; Linda Roberts, director of the U.S. Office of Education Technology under President Clinton; Gwen Solomon, Dr. Roberts' former deputy, and now director of Tech Learning; Lisa Ernst, former director of the ThinkQuest programs and the first director of ThinkQuest NYC; Paris Treantafeles, director of the ANS help desk; Terry Katz, who got us out of jams and continues to do so; Russ Demarest, ThinkQuest NYC tech adviser; Yvonne Andress and Al Rogers from the GlobalSchoolNet, who helped us spread and administer ThinkQuest in the early days; Margaret Riel, a senior researcher at the Center for Technology in Learning at SRI International, and a former researcher into teacher learning at the University of California–Irvine; Beverly Rogers, former director of the Texas Computer Education Association; and Kathy Schrock, a school librarian and media specialist from Nauset, Massachusetts.

I especially want to thank all of the ThinkQuest coaches—with special thanks to those who helped with this book: Neme Alperstein, Rosemary Anderson, Diane Bundy, Carol Calderwood, Don Hyatt, John Lokatos, Hope Mendez, John Payne, Tina Photakis, Bill Reed, Debangsu Sengupta, Yuri and Katrin Shumakov, and Lynn Sueoka.

For their contributions to our international program, I'd like to acknowledge Klaus Rademacher, who was instrumental in founding *Schulen ans Netz* in Germany and promoting ThinkQuest there; Jette Skeem from Denmark; Heba Ramzy and Hisham El Sherif from Egypt; and our other wonderful supporters around the world.

Holly and Jim Brooks were instrumental in promoting Think-Quest in California and in making our awards events in Los Angeles a success. Jacob Gutnicki and the New York City board of education deserve special recognition for their support of ThinkQuest NYC, as do Pamela Trincado, Danielle Mat, and Loretta Torossian.

I also want to thank Dr. Terry Rogers, who for several years helped guide ThinkQuest and ANS and gave his heart to this work.

For their visionary work with ThinkQuest NYC, I'd like to cite Barbara Colwell, Allison Carrabba, Edie Wiener, Eric Orange, and Michael Wehner. And for their continuing sponsorship of Think-Quest, the dedicated people at the Oracle Education Foundation, including Bernard Trilling, Claire Dolan, Collean Cassity, Maya Mirt, and Orla Ni Chorcora. The following ThinkQuest partici-pants responded to our request for interviews and updates and shared their memories of the contest: Mohamed Abdallah, Fatima

Abedin, Sigit Adinugroho, Karandeep Ahluwalia, Muhammad Arif, Elise Boyd, Hillary Calderwood, Miranda Calderwood, Candace Camacho, Kevin Centeno, Rodolfo Chikilicuatre, Joshua Chou, Granite Christopher, Kushal Dave, Victoria Delhoume, Ronald Diu, Mohamed El-Zohairy, Onno Faber, Sytse Faber, Angelicum Fernandez Oda, Brad Galiette, Mayank Gandhi, Charles Gelman, Alyssa Genna, Fabian Gerard, Madelaine Gesslein, Randi Gesslein, Chris Glazer, Ashleigh Green, Harsha Gupta, Rudy Ham-Zu, Ming Han, Jory Hanus, David Hu, Mike Hunigal, Thijs Jacobs, Vimalkumar Jeyakumar, Anmolpreet Kandola, Karmveer Kaur, Sunil Kejariwal, Steve Kessler, Kjersti Kuenle, Alex Kulezsa, Brent Lightner, Pei-Ying Lin, Shawn Low, Gerald McGovern, Patrick Mendez, Brent Metz, Benjamin Meyers, Lorien Miller, Videsh Misir, Manas Mittal, Ahmed Morsi, Michael Muelly, Jaevion Nelson, Keiji Oenoki, Andrew Polyak, Ang Qing Sheng, Shan Rivzi, Wang Ru, Sara Safavi, Yuki Sato, Melissa Sconyers, Parth Shah, Mahmoud Shalaby, Aishwerya Sharma, Suparna Singh, Krishna Sistla, Chip Slate, Galvin Sng, Gee Soon Chee, Gi Soon Kee, Darren Sueoka, Dawn Sueoka, Katie Sullivan, Emilie Sutterlin, Josh Tauberer, Harry Tetteh, Ngoc Tran, Alice Whittington, and Chloe Williams.

A general note of thanks to all those who have participated in ThinkQuest, ThinkQuest International, ThinkQuest Junior, Think-Quest for Tomorrow's Teachers, ThinkQuest NYC, and the many ThinkQuest organizations around the world.

Jaron Lanier led the National Tele-Immersion Initiative and was responsible for the first collaborative effort to develop this new generation of Internet technology. This was a triumph of computer science departments from a number of universities working cooperatively on a big problem. Lanier's team included Amela Sadagic and Marlone Brown at ANS; Andries van Dam and his colleagues at Brown University; Henry Fuchs and his colleagues at the University of North Carolina–Chapel Hill; Ruzena Bajcsy and her colleagues at the University of Pennsylvania; Mychael Zyda and others at the

Naval Postgraduate School in Monterey, California; Steven Feiner at Columbia University; Thomas DeFanti and Maggie Rawlings at the University of Illinois–Urbana-Champaign; and Ulrich Neumann at the University of Southern California.

As we entered the field of philanthropy, we were inspired by the dedication and passion of a number of individuals in the business and high-tech fields who chose to devote their lives to helping others. At Computers for Youth, I would especially like to thank cofounders Elisabeth Stock and Dan Dolgin; director of research Kallen Tsikalis; national development director Janice Goldfarb; master teacher Berkis Cruz Eusebio; and students Diamone Moon and Suleyma Cuellar. At the National Foundation for Teaching Entrepreneurship, special thanks go to Steve Mariotti, the driving force behind the program; the director of NFTE's South Florida program, Alice Horn; Horn's staff, Vanessa Horwell, and her publicists at Think.ink. At Year Up, I want to particularly thank founder Gerald Chertavian for his overview of national antipoverty initiatives and his heart of gold; Doug Borchard, the managing partner and COO of New Profit, who introduced me to Chertavian; and Chertavian's colleagues Kira Intrator and Jay Banfield.

In my hometown of Sarasota, Florida, I'd like to thank Cindy Kaiser, director of the Education Foundation; Mike Horan and Alina Klein of the Sarasota Department of Education, who are the backbone of the TeXellence program; Carlotta Cooley, who introduced me to Ron Zimmerman; and Zimmerman himself, who is the father of getting computers into the homes of kids who need them in Sarasota; Dave Winkelman, past president of PC Users Group; and my former CFO Bob Harris, who remains active in this organization.

I extend my deep appreciation again to all ANS officers and board members for their years of service and their willingness to help evolve a technology company into an educational force and then embrace a new kind of philanthropy. For giving of their time and expertise, I thank: Joe Dionne, former chairman and CEO of McGraw-Hill, who helped us transition from a high-tech company to a global educational network through his hard questions; Myra Williams, who led us to support Princeton Young Achievers; Jim McGroddy, who has always been there for the first wave of advice, who convinced me to write this book, and who introduced us to the Cristo Rey network of schools, with their innovative work-study approach; John Armstrong, who took a big risk and convinced IBM to change their direction in network products; Richard West, California State University executive vice chancellor, and his associate Laurie Redfearn, who encouraged us to fund TELACU, now the nation's largest community development project; and TELACU's visionary CEO, Michael Lizzaraga. Richard West also pointed us to John Gersuk, director of government affairs for the JASON Project, who described the program's evolution and its new curriculum; Joe B. Wyatt, chancellor emeritus of Vanderbilt University, who provided an inside view of the educational system; Gerry Butters, former president of Northern Telecom, who helped save ANS at a time when it nearly broke the golden rule of business—"never run out of cash"; Armando Garcia, vice president of technical strategy and worldwide operations for IBM Research, who has supported our efforts and helped us along the way; and Kristin Mortensen, my assistant for twenty-five-plus years, a wonderful person who has always been there to tell me where to go. She has calmly paid the bills and, as she duly noted, "watched so many worthy projects grow."

Finally, heartiest thanks to my coauthor, Valerie Andrews, who put up with me through this long but wonderful process of giving birth to a book. She is a master of weaving hundreds of scraps of paper, minutes of board meetings, and interviews into a suspenseful narrative.

NOTES

1. Statistics on American students not being up to par in math and science were taken from the Education Wonks blogsite, December 6, 2007, in an article titled "U.S. Students Not Comparing Well with Others" (available at http://educationwonk.blogspot.com/2007/12/us-students-not-comparing-well-with.html); and *New York Times*, November 14, 2007, in an article titled "Study Compares States' Math and Science Scores with Other Count" (available at http://www.nytimes.com/2007/11/14/education/14students.html). See also the proceedings of the Woodrow Wilson International Center for Scholars online conference, November 14, 2007, titled "Math and Science Teaching in Northeast Asia: Do They Do It Better?" (available at http://www.wilsoncenter.org/index.cfm?topic_id=1408&fuseaction=topics.event_summary&event_id=297769).

2. For additional information, see *Rising Above the Gathering Storm: Energizing and Employing America for a Brighter Future* (Washington, D.C.: National Academies Press, 2007).

3. James McGroddy's essay, "Raising Mice in an Elephant's Cage," originally appeared in *Taking Technical Risks: How Innovators, Executives, and Investors Manage High-Tech Risks*, ed. Lewis M. Branscomb and Philip E. Auerswald (Cambridge, MA: MIT Press, 2001). It is available at http://www.hks.harvard.edu/sed/docs/k4dev/mcgroddy_techrisk_2001.pdf.

4. http://www.techterms.com.

5. Hearing on the National Science Foundation Network, U.S. House of Representatives Subcommittee on Science, March 12, 1992. Comments from CIX members and telecommunications representatives are contained here as well.

6. In 1994, the U.S. government had just completed its first survey of computer use in public schools. For more information, see "Internet Access in U.S. Public Schools and Classrooms: 1994–2000" (available at http://nces.ed.gov/pubsearch/pubsinfo.asp?pubid=2001071).

7. See Howard E. Gardner, *Frames of Mind: The Theory of Multiple Intelligences*, 10th ed. (New York: Basic Books, 1993).

8. See the CEO Forum's "Report on Technology and Education," 1997 (available at http://www.ceoforum.org/downloads/forum3.pdf).

9. U.S. Educational Resources Information Center, ED424383— *Communication on Computer: Improving Reading and Writing Skills Using a Computer.* Instructor's Guide. Workplace Education. Project ALERT (available at http://www.eric.ed.gov).

10. *The University Record* (a publication of the University of Michigan), October 28, 1998, "Computer-Aided Collaboration Builds Writing Skills" (available at http://www.ur.umich.edu/9899/Oct28_98/9.htm). This article describes a research project on writing and computer skills begun at the university in 1995.

11. "The 1997 National Survey of U.S. Public Libraries and the Internet." The report was prepared for the Office for Information Technology Policy at the American Library Association (available at http://userpages.umbc.edu/~bertot/ala97.html).

12. Press release from the U.S. Department of Education, "Secretary of Education Riley and CEO Forum Challenge Higher Ed to Provide New Teachers with Technology Skills," January 10, 2000. Available in the online archives at http://www.ed.gov/PressReleases/01-2000/skills.html.

13. For a complete account of our early experiments with tele-immersion, see Jaron Lanier's article "Virtually There" in the April 2001 issue of *Scientific American.*

14. For more on this subject, see Jaron Lanier's article "I Smell, Therefore I Think," in *Discover* magazine (available at http://discovermagazine. com/2006/may/jarons-world).

15. Karen Kaplan, "A Virtual World Is Taking Shape in Research Labs Technology: The Internet of the Future Will Surround Users with Sights, Sounds, Even Smells," *Los Angeles Times*, February 5, 2001 (available at http://articles.latimes.com/2001/feb/05/business/fi-21375).

16. For more information about Cybergrasp, see the University of Southern California website on immersive technology (available at http://imsc.usc.edu/haptics/).

17. The Children's Data Bank maintains statistics on dropouts and their family demographics (available at http://www.childtrendsdatabank. org/indicators/1HighSchoolDropout.cfm).

18. "One-Third of a Nation: Rising Dropout Rates and Declining Opportunities," report published by the Educational Testing Service (available at http://www.ets.org/Media/Education_Topics/pdf/ onethird.pdf).

19. Cliff Hakim, *We Are All Self-Employed: How To Take Control of Your Career.* (San Francisco: Berrett-Koehler, 2003).

20. For more information on the IFTF report, see "Generation Y Creates the Age of Entrepreneurship" (available at http://www.mba.co.za/ article.aspx?rootid=6&subdirectoryid=1333).

21. The article "Some Orders That the Boss Should Heed," *New York Times*, December 27, 2007, describes the work of Cathleen Benko at Deloitte and Touche USA (available at http://www.nytimes. com/2007/12/27/fashion/27Work.html?scp=1&sq=corporate+lattice& st=nyt).

RESOURCES

I. Building the Backbone of the Internet

The **Computer History Museum** (http://www.computerhistory.org) contains a fascinating time line of the computer. Their collection shows the contributions made by individual companies, a history of components and technical innovations, a view of people and pop culture (who discovered the first computer bug, for example), as well as a history of networking and information on the evolution of games, robots, and artificial intelligence.

Archives from the **Twentieth Anniversary Conference on the National Science Foundation Network**, held in November 2007, are available at http://www.nsfnet-legacy.org/archive.

II. An Educational Olympics on the Web

Apple Computer Education (http://www.apple.com/education/) is a valuable resource for students and teachers using Mac software and computers. Apple also provides discounts for school programs.

Edutopia (http://www.edutopia.org) is a rich online resource provided by the George Lucas Educational Foundation (GLEF). A storyteller for education, GLEF profiles how teachers and students around the country are enacting many inspiring stories and transforming their schools. The site includes a video library and case histories of exciting tech learning projects.

The **U.S. Department of Education** (http://www.ed.gov/Technology/eratemenu.html) offers discounts (E-Rate programs) on Internet use for schools and libraries.

E-School News (http://www.eschoolnews.com) is the K–12 decision maker's technology and Internet newspaper, covering policy issues, trends in tech education, and the latest research in tech ed.

Microsoft Education (http://www.microsoft.com/education) offers lesson plans, tutorials, and in-depth Microsoft product resources, including Office and Windows, for K–12 and higher education.

Tech Learning (http://www.techlearning.com), run by Gwen Solomon, offers a rich compendium of print and online resources for educators. *Technology & Learning Magazine* produced this site with contributions from hundreds of K–12 teachers, administrators, and other experts in the field.

Tele-immersion will lead us to the "Classroom of the Future." This leading-edge technology allows us to combine virtual worlds with reality. For more information on the latest developments in this field, see:

UC Berkeley Lab at http://tele-immersion.citris-uc.org/.

USC Haptics Program at http://imsc.usc.edu/haptics/projects.html.

University of North Carolina at http://imsc.usc.edu/haptics/projects.html.

Brown University at http://graphics.cs.brown.edu/research/telei/.

University of Illinois at http://www.isl.uiuc.edu/canvas/evafirenze08.ppt.

Achives: The May and October 2000 demonstrations of tele-immersion can be found online at http://www.advanced.org/tele-immersion/news.html.

For more information about the global tech education programs **ThinkQuest** and **Think.com**, go to www.thinkquest.org. This site contains information for students, parents, teachers, and school administrators. The ThinkQuest Library is the world's largest online resource, housing more than seven thousand educational websites that were created by ThinkQuest students.

ThinkQuest NYC (http://www.tqnyc.org) has now expanded into the greater metropolitan area of New York. This competition also includes a special award for websites that focus on supporting charitable organizations.

III. What Is Reality?

Computers for Youth (http://www.cfy.org) helps low-income children do better in school by improving their environment at home. Our nation is failing to provide low-income children the support they need during the critical middle school years. As a result, test scores are dropping sharply between the fifth and sixth grades. School-based efforts to address this challenge have fallen short. Children spend only 13 percent of their waking hours in the classroom.

CFY offers an innovative solution with proven results. It improves student achievement by enhancing the educational resources available in children's homes, by improving parent-child interaction around learning, and by helping teachers make powerful links between the classroom and the home. This organization now has offices in New York, Philadelphia, Atlanta, the San Francisco Bay Area, and Los Angeles. In addition, CFY has launched an affiliate network that reaches out to schools in all fifty U.S. states.

The **Cristo Rey Schools** (http://www.cristorey.org) provide a unique work-study program for low-income students and also teach the value of giving back though community service. There are now twenty-one schools, nineteen in urban areas across the United States. For more information about their mission, read *More Than a Dream: How One School's Vision Is Changing the World*, published by Loyola Press. To meet students from Cristo Rey New York, log onto the website and watch the video.

The **Education Foundation of Sarasota TeXcellence Program** (http://
www.srqk12.net/TeXcellence/testclassicpage.aspx) helps low-income
families in Sarasota County, Florida, by following many of the concepts embodied in Computers for Youth.

The **JASON Project** (http://www.jason.org) is a nonprofit subsidiary of the National Geographic Society, connecting young students
with great explorers to inspire them to pursue careers in science. Its
core curriculum units are designed for fifth- through eighth- grade
classrooms, but they are flexible enough to be adapted for higher
or lower grades. Throughout the year, JASON gives every student
a number of opportunities to join real expeditions without leaving
their classrooms.

The **National Foundation for Teaching Entrepreneurship** (http://
www.nfte.com) helps young people from low-income communities
build skills and unlock their entrepreneurial creativity. Since 1987,
NFTE has reached more than 186,000 young people, and it currently
has programs in twenty-one states and thirteen countries. NFTE has
more than a thousand active Certified Entrepreneurship Teachers,
and it is continually improving its innovative entrepreneurship curriculum. For more information about the curriculum, read Steve Mariotti's *How to Start and Operate a Small Business*, now in its ninth
revised edition. (The book is available through NFTE's website.)

Princeton Young Achievers (http://www.princetonyoungachievers.org)
helps children from low- and moderate-income neighborhoods improve
their school performance and English language skills. Every Monday
through Friday, Princeton K–5 schoolchildren meet at neighborhood
centers for homework support and enrichment activities including science and art projects, one-on-one tutoring, and literacy support.

TELACU (http://www.TELACU.com) is a pioneering institution committed to service and to the empowerment of the Hispanic community
in Los Angeles. Chartered as a Community Development Corpora-

tion, TELACU was funded through federal legislation sponsored by senators Robert F. Kennedy and Jacob K. Javits. Its goal: to revitalize urban, underserved communities throughout the United States.

Every business TELACU owns and operates has a double bottom line—profitability that is inseparable from social impact. For-profit businesses not only provide valuable products and services to the community, they also provide the economic means for TELACU to sustain its nonprofit community-focused entities. Quality, affordable homes are developed for first-time homeowners, and beautiful residential complexes are constructed and operated for families and senior citizens. New community assets like schools, infrastructure, shopping centers, and municipal facilities are built, creating well-paying jobs and revitalized communities for local residents. Responsive financial institutions are managed to provide access to capital for small-business owners and hardworking families, and educational opportunities are expanded to create a greater future for young people and veterans.

Telepresence (http://www.jason.org) is now embedded in the JASON Project's inquiry-based curriculum through videos, podcasts, webcasts, live chat sessions, and interactive computer simulations—all aligned to national science standards and seamlessly integrated into the framework of a four-color, magazine-style print curriculum.

Year Up (http://www.yearup.org) is a one-year intensive training program that provides urban young adults, ages eighteen to twenty-four, with a combination of hands-on skill development, college credits, and corporate apprenticeships.

During the first six months of the program, participants focus on skill mastery in one of two areas: (1) Desktop Support/IT Help Desk; or (2) Investment Operations. Equal emphasis is placed on developing the professional skills—such as effective communication, leadership, and teamwork—required in today's workplace.

During the second six months of the program, students are placed in apprenticeships with local partner companies. A stipend is provided to all participants throughout the one-year, full-time educational program.

With offices in Atlanta, Boston, New York City, Providence, San Francisco, and Washington, Year Up will soon expand to other urban areas across the country.

IV. Social Entrepreneurs

Ashoka (http://www.ashoka.org) is a global association of the world's leading social entrepreneurs—men and women with system-changing solutions for the world's most urgent social problems. Since 1981, this organization has identified and supported more than two thousand leading social entrepreneurs. These Ashoka Fellows receive living stipends, professional support, and access to a global network of peers in more than sixty countries.

This global community develops models for collaboration and designs infrastructure needed to advance the field of social entrepreneurship and the citizen sector. Ashoka Fellows inspire others to adopt and spread their innovations, demonstrating to all citizens that they, too, have the potential to be powerful change makers.

New Profit (http://newprofit.com) is a national venture philanthropy organization that helps visionary social entrepreneurs and their organizations bring about widespread and transformative impact on critical social problems. New Profit works to fulfill this mission using two approaches: (1) it provides financial and strategic support to selected social entrepreneurs and their organizations; and (2) it helps build an environment that enables all social entrepreneurs and their organizations to transform their communities.

INDEX